TO BE OR NOT TO BE
SUDAN AT CROSSROADS

A Pan-African Perspective

A black African nation
undone by the ideology
of Islamo-Arabism

TO BE OR NOT TO BE
SUDAN AT CROSSROADS

A Pan-African Perspective

A black African nation
undone by the ideology
of Islamo-Arabism

M. Jalāl Hāshim

MKUKI NA NYOTA
DAR-ES-SALAAM

Published by
Mkuki na Nyota Publishers Ltd
P. O. Box 4246
Dar es Salaam, Tanzania
www.mkukinanyota.com

ISBN 978-9987-083-76-3

Visit www.mkukinanyota.com to read more about and to purchase any of Mkuki na Nyota books. You will also find featured authors interviews and news about other publisher/author events. Sign up for our e-newsletters for updates on new releases and other announcements.

Distributed worldwide outside Africa by African Books Collective.
www.africanbookscollective.com

Contents

To John Garang de Mabior and Bankie F. Bankie

Our hands will burst the galling chain
Our people will be free again
For them a thousand hopes remain
(Modified from a poem by Emily Brontë)

Preface to "To Be or Not to Be: Sudan at Crossroads"

I have been an avid reader of the work of M. Jalal Hashim (MJH) for about a decade. This is the first time I read a book of his in English.

For me, as a Sudanese reader and writer, MJH has a firm place in a special, short list of critically important, contemporary Sudanese writers, due to his prolific and valuable record of publications, mostly in Arabic (with some papers and essays in English), addressing various topics from Sudan's social history, to political theory, to cultural analysis and literary critique. I am elated that his well-thought and enduring theorization about the Sudanese predicament will be, at last, more accessible to English readers.

MJH establishes the realm of culture (defined holistically) as the basis of his proposal for understanding the problem(s) of post-colonial Sudan. A significant majority of the Sudanese people, MJH argues, suffer from a peculiar, chronic and severe cultural identity crisis. That crisis was a result of a cultural fallacy that emerged due to local peculiarities before colonization, amplified in the colonial era, and has been reproduced ever since. That continuous process works for the benefit of an elite, minority 'centre' through monopolization of power and wealth to the extreme disadvantage of the country's majority populations on 'the margins'. Both the centre and margins are defined objectively, in this thesis, on basis of power and wealth concentration, instead of fluid or arbitrary ethno-geographic definitions. The centre uses particular, valuable components of Sudan's large multicultural mosaic – Islam (or 'Islamdom') and Arabic heritage – as ideological tools for reproducing itself, desecrating both components in the process while simultaneously marginalizing all the other components. This Islamo-Arab ideology desecrates both Islam and Arabic heritage by deforming both, from their natural state as genuine cultural components among several others in Sudan, to become tools of exclusion of "the others" from power and wealth. Hence, even as the two cultural components are not put on trial themselves, in this thesis, what is under scrutiny is how the centre manipulates them for its own interests.

In reality, the only logical and inclusive national identity for Sudan, capable of bringing its various cultural components in cohesion, connecting its magnificent and complex history to its present, and unlocking the potential of the people and the land, is the African identity, MJH argues. It is a general historical, social and political identity that is consistent with the objective realities in Sudan. It does not exclude anyone, and it opens broader cultural possibilities than any other proposed national identity. In that light, MJH proposes Pan-Africanism as a way for Sudanese intellectuals and social movements to reconnect with Africa and its nations.

MJH, and other Sudanese intellectuals who agree with him, assert that understanding the centre-margin conflict in Sudan illuminates the historical forces at work in the country and helps in resolving the crises it creates, thereby ushering a way out of the vicious cycle of injustice, instability, war and underdevelopment.

MJH does an impressive job in this book by using language and style that make the exposition of his controversial thesis easily accessible to his audiences in and out of Sudan. It is undoubtedly his most significant contribution to Sudanese socio-political thought from a Pan-Africanist perspective. This book is highly recommended for all those interested in making sense of the complex phenomenon that is contemporary Sudan/South Sudan.

Gussai Sheikheldin
September 2018, Dar es Salaam
Author of *Liberation and Technology* and *As'Sulta Al'Khamisa* (the fifth Estate)

CHAPTER 1

Introduction

1.1. Sudan: the Name

The name "Sudan" has more or less been the same throughout history. Aside from the toponyms relating to the south (such as *Hent-Hen-Nefer* and *Wawat*), it has been associated with the colour of blackness, such as '*Ta-Nehesu*', '*Kush*', '*Kerma*', '*Æthiopia*', '*Nubia*', '*al-Salṭana* al-Zarga' and last but not least '*al-Sūdān*' (Sagheiroun, 1999). This continuum, which starts from the early time of the ancient civilizations of the Nile valley up to the present, has reflected the colour of its people. The same name seems to have evolved by translation from one language to another in the course of time. This, regarding belonging and identity, puts Sudan in the heart of Africa, which is rightly called the Black Continent. What appear to be differences of colour among the Sudanese are nothing more than just different shades of blackness.

The significance of the name "Sūdān" is crucially important, because it bears very strong identity implications. The Arabized people of middle Sudan, generally speaking, tend not to recognize themselves as black Africans. As the state for the last five centuries has functionally belonged to the ideology of this Arabized group, Sudan has ended up identifying with Arabs much more than with black Africa.

This issue of identity is deemed central in the contemporary problem of self-actualization of Sudan in particular and in national integration in general. Sudanese people are either bearers of a name unfit for them or a name that they do not deserve. It is a doomed person who bears a name that does not satisfy their self-esteem. Since independence in 1956, the state has evasively dealt with the realistic connotations and implications of the name "Sudan" without ever trying to ground it in the psyche of the Sudanese youngsters in educational curricula. Ironically, a poem by the Lebanese poet Iliya Abu Māḍi (cf. http://www.taamolatadab.com/) that deplores blackness was once taught in our schools. The poem, titled "Florida", speaks about the American state "Florida" and is named after it. It praises the city's natural and human beauties while deprecating its black people describing them as flies among roses; praising its natrual beauty and that of its inhabitants, he mentions the only exception is its black coloured people:

Everything that appeared on its land is beautiful;

All of the best is what appears in the eyes of its people,

If only it were not for those of black colour;

Alas! A garden with flies around its edges!

It's soul-destroying for my eye to see them and see the young ladies.

Needless to say, some of the gruesome racist novels about Africa written by racist Western writers were also among the books of English literature taught in our schools.

No wonder in their Western diaspora, the particular Sudanese who have fallen victim to this self-alienation choose the category "Other" in identifying themselves instead of any of the following categories: "White", "Arab", "Asian" or "Black" (for more details about a particular incident that took place in Britain, cf. Afif, 2002). The last category "Blacks" includes the sub-category "Africans". By not recognizing themselves as blacks, they not only deprived themselves of the honour of being Africans, but also contradicted the simple truths of reality. At the same time they could not dare call themselves Arabs while living in the West - an identity they always boast of while they are inside the Sudan. By opting to be neither "Africans" nor "Arabs", they remained in the obscurity of the non-identity of "Otherness".

1.2. The State

The State has prevailed throughout history in what roughly constitutes the geography of present day two Sudans. Archaeologically, the state can be traced back for at least seven thousand years (cf. Welsby, 2000). As in other parts of Africa, the state functioned in a kind of federal autonomy where the ethno-cultural entities were its political nucleuses. The vast geographical space necessitated that justice became a cornerstone of the foundations for any ruler to stay in power. Every ethnic group was at liberty to seek a better place to live and settle in, which would leave any tyrant to preside only over the desert or jungle. Using today's modern language, a typical traditional African "democracy" prevailed where both the supremacy of the ruler and the autonomy of the groups of subjects were acknowledged. The ancient civilizations of Nubia were characterized by this just equilibrium of freedom and sovereignty.

Comparatively, it was the opposite in the sisterly civilization of ancient Egypt, where rulers maintained absolute power over their subjects. As the people there were confined to the narrow strip of the Nile by the hedging desert, they became vulnerable to the supremacy of their rulers. From then, unpaid compulsory work was introduced, only to be abolished by 'Abdu al-Nāṣir in the mid-20th century. The vast human resources available as a result may well be the reason behind the successful construction of huge monuments and pyramids. However, in ancient Nubia, the ruler could not compel the subjects into such work – a factor that may explain why Sudan ended up with relatively humble pyramids in comparison. Today's demand for self-determination by different marginalized groups is the modern manifestation and formulation of the history-long practice of pulling out from any state that does not respond equally to the longing of its different subject-groups for freedom, justice and peace.

At no time was there any kind of political vacuum in the Sudan. The traditional tribal federacy of ancient Nubia, which was maintained in the Christian era (650AD-1505AD), would later also prevail in the Funj sultanate (1505AD-1821AD). The Turco-Egyptian colonial rule (1821AD-1885AD) is wrongly thought to have introduced the policy of decentralization in ruling the Sudan; in fact it was the same ancient system that was applied in the Funj sultanate and then reinstated later. The realities of pluralism in Sudan have always pushed the state towards adopting decentralized and federal policies. It is a continuum that goes back thousands of years.

1.3. The People

Virtually all the people of present-day Sudan have contributed to making the ancient civilization of Nubia. Sometimes this civilization is called "Nubian", but this should be understood in the way of "naming the part while meaning the whole". Even the people who call themselves

"Arab" have the right to a recognizable share in the construction of that civilization due to their ancestral roots, a mixture of Arabs and indigenous people. In fact the weaving of the ethno-linguistic fabric in Sudan, which is taken for granted to be heterogeneous, reflects homogeneity as well. Amazingly people living on the Sudan-Uganda borders (e.g. the Baria) have a 'cousin' kinship with people living on the Sudan-Egypt borders (Nubians) and both people are related to others living on the Sudan-Ethiopia borders in the Funj region (e.g. South Blue Nile). All of these groups are related in the same way to other groups living on the Sudan-Chad borders (e.g. Daju). This will look natural when one bears in mind that before the Arabization of middle Sudan those people were in dynamic contact with each other. This is an ancient land with ancient people and an ancient civilization; therefore not surprising that they are interrelated ethno-linguistically.

The peoples of Africa are generally classified ethno-linguistically into four big groups (phyla), namely: Afro-Asiatic, Niger-Kordofanian, Nilo-Saharan, and Khoi-San. Only the last phylum is not represented in the Sudan by any ethno-linguistic group as it is confined to the southern tail of the continent. Each phylum is divided into sub-groups and smaller groups until it reaches the level of the sisterly ethno-linguistic entities, or families, in a way almost similar to the kinship trees of the people themselves. For instance, within the Nilo-Saharan we have respectively the Western, Central and Eastern Sudanic sub-groups.

The above-mentioned classification was born out of the racial bigotry and prejudice that characterized Western academia when dealing with Africa. Furthermore, as is usually the case in social sciences, most of the premises and criteria for classification are controversial. This is why African scientists in their UNESCO's General History of Africa came into sharp disagreement with Western scholars regarding the issue of classification. For instance, Westerners classified ancient Egyptians as Afro-Asiatic (thus relating them to the Semitic people), but they were re-classified by the African scientists as Niger-Kordofanian. Some of the Africans even went as far as arguing that what is called Nilo-Saharan could constitute one bigger group with the so-called Niger-Kordofanian (cf. Ki-Zerbo, 1989).

Bearing in mind the above-mentioned controversy, we will allow ourselves to adopt that classification, as it is still widely being taught in African academia. Below we are going to show how the peoples of the Sudan are related to each other in an intrinsic way. The ethno-linguistic groups will be mentioned according to their principal regional habitats, which comprise the following (prior to the secession of South Sudan): Equatoria, Bahr al-Ghazal, South Upper Nile, Nuba Mountains, Darfur, Funj and South Blue Nile, Eastern Sudan, Northern Sudan, and Middle Sudan (cf. www.ethnologue.org). The languages spoken by the people in these areas will be used as an indicator of the ethnic groups. Now, with the intensification of marginalization, people have moved away from their historical habitats to other areas, mainly the middle of the country. This classification will not be strictly considered in all cases. Although Arabic, being the lingua franca of the Sudan, is spoken all over the country, it will be related to the middle of Sudan where it claims supremacy. "Northern Sudan" indicates here the ethno-linguistically distinguishable group of Nubians exclusively. Both Meroitic and Old Nubian and other extinct languages will be mentioned for historical significance only. The Nuba Mountains represent the whole of Kordofan as, aside from Arabic, there is only one language that falls outside Nuba Mountains, i.e. the extinct Ḥarāza language. The ethno-linguistic affiliation will be marked by the following characters, which are randomly applied: Afro-Asiatic (☺); Congo-Kordofanian (♂); and Nilo-Saharan (☼) with its sub-group of Eastern Sudanic as (♀). This symbol (☻) indicates that almost all the languages are spoken in the given area. The eastern Sudanic sub-group will be mentioned because it cuts across the country, from Nimuli (bordering with Uganda) to Halfa (bordering with Egypt), and from al-Jinēna (bordering Chad) to al-Kurmuk (bordering Ethiopia). We shall try to mention all ethnic entities, but we cannot claim that the list is inclusive. Apology is due to those whose languages have not been mentioned. Bearing in mind the huge number of Sudanese languages (over 400 ones including dialects), one can expect some to slip from record. The alphabetic order will be adopted.

1.3.1. Middle Sudan

☺ Arabic Colloquial
☺ Arabic Standard
♀ Meroitic
♀ Old Nubian
☻ All

1.3.2. Eastern Sudan

☺ Arabic
☺ Bedaweyit
♂ Fulani
☼ Fur
☺ Hausa
♀ Meroitic

♀ Nobíin ♀ Old Nubian ☺ Tigrey
☺ Tigrinya

1.3.3. Northern Sudan

☺ Arabic ♀ Dongolese ♀ Kunūz
♀ Meroitic ♀ Nobíin ♀ Old Nubian

1.3.4. The Nuba Mountains and Kordofan

♀ Affitti ♀ Aka ♀ Ama
☺ Arabic ♂ Dagik ♀ Dair
♀ Daju ♀ Delenj ♀ Dinka
♂ Eliri ♂ Fulani ♂ Garme
♀ Ḥugairat ♀ Ghulfān ♀ Ḥaraza
☺ Hausa ♂ Heiban ♀ Kadaru
♀ Kanga ♀ Karko ♀ Katcha
♂ Kadugli ♂ Katla ♂ Keiga
♂ Kawalib ♀ Kau ♂ Korongo
♂ Lafofa ♂ Laru ♀ Liguri
♂ Logol ♂ Lumun ♀ Meroitic
♂ Moro ♂ Ngile ♀ Old Nubian
♀ Shatt ♂ Shuway ♂ Tagoi
♂ Talodi ♀ Tese ♀ Temain
♀ Tima ♂ Tingal ♂ Tocho
♂ Togole ♂ Torona ♂ Tulishi
♀ Tumma ♂ Utoro ♀ Wali
♂ Warnag ☼ Yulu

1.3.5. Darfur

☺ Arabic ☼ Bargo ♀ Baygo
☼ Berti ♀ Birgid ♀ Berno

♀ Daju	☼ Fongoro	♂ Fulani
☼ Fur	☺ Hausa	♀ Kanuri
☼ Masalit	♀ Meroitic	♀ Midob
♀ Old Nubian	♀ Sungor	☼ Zaghawa

1.3.6. Bahr al Ghazāl

☼ Ajja	☺ Arabic	♀ Daju
♀ Dinka	♂ Feroge	♂ Fulani
☼ Gula	☺ Hausa	♂ Mangayat
♀ Meroitic	☼ Mittu	♀ Njalgulgule
♀ Old Nubian	☼ Sinyar	

1.3.7. Equatoria

☼ Abukeia	♀ Acholi	☺ Arabic Std.
☺ Arabic Juba	♂ Bai	☼ Baka
♂ Banda	♀ Baria	♀ Belanda Bor
♂ Belanda Viri	☼ Bongo	♀ Dongotono
♂ Homa	♂ Indri	☼ Jur
♀ Kachipo	♀ Kakwa	☼ Kaliko
☼ Kresh	♀ Lango	♀ Lokoya
♀ Lopit	☼ Luluba	♀ Luwo
☼ Ma'adi	♀ Mundari	♀ Meroitic
☼ Mo'da	☼ Morokodo	☼ Moru
♂ Mundo	♂ Ndogo	☼ Njamusa
☼ Molo	♀ Old Nubian	♀ Otuho
♀ Shilluk	♀ Suri	♀ Tennet
♀ Thuri	♂ Togoyo	♀ Toposa
♂ Zande		

1.3.8. Upper Nile

♀ Anuak	☺ Arabic	♀ Atuot
☼ Beli	♀ Didinga	♀ Dinka
♀ Jumjum	♀ Lokoro	♀ Longarim
♀ Mabaan	♀ Meroitic	♀ Murle
♀ Nuer	♀ Old Nubian	♂ Tumtum
☼ Uduk		

1.3.9. Upper Blue Nile

☺ Arabic	☼ Berta	♀ Burun
♂ Fulani	☼ Funj	☼ Gumuz
☺ Hausa	♀ Ingassana	♀ Kelo
☼ Komo	♀ Meroitic	♀ Molo
♀ Old Nubian	☼ Opuuo	

1.3.10. The Stereotype of the Linear Cut: North vs. South

The above-mentioned relationships, which reflect the reality of today, stand as evidence that the Sudanese people are united in their diversity. How can one draw a line and say that this is the South and this is the North? Or even this is the East and this is the West? All the groups cut across the country from Ḥalfa to Nimuli and from Kurmuk to Jinēna. The Nilo-Saharan Group (☼), of which the Eastern Sudanic (♀) is a sub-group, constitutes 64% of the total identities of the Sudan; of the Nilo-Saharan phylum, the Eastern Sudanic sub-group (♀) alone constitutes 44% of its phylum and 22% of the total number of identities in the two Sudans. The Congo-Kordofanian Group (♂) constitutes 32%, where the Afro-Asiatic Group (☺) constitutes only 4%. Although the populations of these ethnic identities are proportionately reversed, the issue of human rights, however, is not a question of "how many?" All ethnic groups are entitled to equal rights in matters pertaining to culture and development regardless of whether their population number is small or big.

1.4. The Boundary

The historic boundaries of ancient Sudan are thought to have been much bigger than today's boundaries. The chart of languages shows that all areas share the Meroitic and Old Nubian languages. Consequently their culture and civilization are also shared. There is archaeological evidence to this effect. Excavations have proved that there are both Cushitic/Meroitic and Post-Meroitic settlements in Southern, Western and Eastern regions. The linguistic evidence is proving that languages as far as Equatoria (the Baria (♀) for instance) can potentially help in deciphering the Meroitic language (♀) ('Abdu al-Gādir M. 'Abdu Allah, 1985). Archaeological evidence has supported the stories of ancient historians about the tall and very black cattle herdsmen who used to roam the area of today's Buṭāna up to the Red Sea Hills. This is also supported by the oral traditions of the Nilotic tribes, the Dinka in particular (cf. Lazarus Leek Mawut, 1983). The meaning of the name "Khartoum", which is traditionally pronounced as "khērtūm" is offered in the Dinka language as "kēr tom", i.e. the "the river confluence" (*ibid*). Just 250 years ago the White Nile region above Jabal Aulia (45 km upstream along the White Nile from Khartoum) was Shillukland. The Arab thrust into the centre of Sudan caused the Nilotic people and other groups to shrink back deep into the Savannah and Equatorial zones, where they got cut off from the milieu of their lingo-cultural setting of the Nilo-Saharan and Niger-Kordofanian regions, which has been in fact disrupted altogether by this factor. The historical and natural frontiers of this region are the equator in the south downstream to the 1st cataract of Asuan in present-day Egypt.

Westward the boundaries of ancient Sudan are much bigger as natural topographical features do not obstruct the movement of people. Recent researches (cf. Lobban et al, 1999) have shown that the iron industry of Meroe is to be associated with the industry of iron smelting in Central *Bilād al-Sūdān* not with the iron industry in the regions north of Sudan. Some Sudanese tribes (al-Daju in particular) show cultural attachment to hills rich with iron ore. The west-east routes between the Red Sea and the Atlantic Ocean were witness to constant migrations on both fronts. The Nubians who have settled in Darfur, Kordofan, and the Nile are generally believed by scholars to have migrated originally from a place north-west of Darfur (cf. Adams, 1982). The Hausa and Fulani people have been taking these routes in their eastward movement since ancient times (El-Nagger, 1970). These are the same routes the

Arabs took in their migration into the Sudan from *Bilād al-Maghrib* and Andalusia (Fadl, 1073). This is why the area that lies between the Red Sea and the Atlantic Ocean is rightly called *Bilād al-Sūdān*, which really constitutes the strategic depth of the Sudan (cf. Fadl, 1971). This is why also countries like Chad used to bear the name "*Sūdān*". Ironically the government of Sudan officially complained when the newly independent Republic of Mali expressed its intention to adopt the name "Sūdān". One would expect such a government to also piously to reverence the semantic connotation and implication of the name.

1.5. Religion

Two things have characterized Sudan throughout history - it has always been multi-religious as well as religiously tolerant. Ancient polytheism accommodated other deities surviving in today's traditional religions. Recent studies in Nubiology trace monotheism back to Nubia. Akhenaton must have developed monotheism before he assumed the throne. If the notion that he was in Nubia (presumably his mother's homeland) in his youth before being called to Egypt to assume the throne is correct, then it was there he had discovered monotheism (Bell & Hāshim, 2002). Tolerant Nubia enabled the development of Akhenaton's monotheism, while intolerant Egypt brought its demise. Evidence of this tolerance could be seen in the fact that the treasurer of the Candace of Meroe (800BC-450AD) was a Jew who converted to Christianity in its early days, apparently without fearing the slightest persecution. Christianity did not invade Nubia (Vantini, 1978; Werner et al, 2000); it was the Nubians who asked for it. In Dongola, the capital of the Christian Kingdom of Nubia (650AD-1350AD), there was a mosque for which the Christian state was responsible. In Soba (circa 20 km upstream along the Blue Nile from Khartoum), the capital of the Christian Kingdom of Alodia (650AD-1505AD), where there were about 300 churches, there was also a mosque within a hamlet designated for the Muslims.

In the 19th century Christianity would catch up again as a result of intensive missionary work. The biggest Christian communities are in the South, Nuba Mountains, South Blue Nile respectively and the big urban centres. In the face of the rise of Islamization and Arabization as vehicles for facilitating the domination of the central state, Christianity got involved and eventually became, along with Africanism, the ideological backbone in countering Islamo-Arabism.

1.5.1. Islam

Islam broke the encapsulation of Sudan in the 16th century and opened it to the world of that time. The transformation from Christianity to Islam was a gradual process thus giving way for a distinctive mix of Sudanese cosmology and a culture of tolerance. A Sudanese Islam was in the making and finally took its shape in the Sufi sects that flourished in Sudan, thus bringing about an effective acculturation of indigenous practices and Islamic teachings. The local people experienced a smooth transition from the traditional and Christian choirs to the Sufi chanting.

The conversion to Islam culminated in the Funj Sultanate (1505AD-1820AD), which retained many ancient features in regard to administration and cultural symbols (cf. Spaulding, 1980). The traditional system of tribal federacy, with its inherent democratic practices, was maintained. Other ancient practices, such as the ritual killing of the king (regicide) and the Christian headgear and regalia, were also retained. At the beginning, Sufi Islam assumed supremacy in reflecting the ideology of the State. A little later, a rival came onto the scene, as represented by fundamentalist Islam that could only be acquired through classroom teaching at such religious centres as al-Azhar in Cairo (Yaḥia Ibrāhīm, 1980). Where Sufi popular Islam interacts with the local society, fundamentalist Islam challenges it in its persistent endeavours to reshape it according to its own norms. Where the former does not give heed to the penal code of the Sharī'a as literally stated in the scriptures, the latter only pays attention to the scriptures without giving any heed to the realities of setting and context. In the beginning many fundamentalist sheikhs took to denouncing their jurisprudence by throwing away their symbolic scholastic graduation robes, to declare themselves as Sufi. At the end of the game this would be reversed.

Sufi popular Islam could have won the rivalry if it had not been for the Turco-Egyptian colonial rule (1820AD-1885AD), which introduced the culture of official Muslim clergymen who were appointed and paid by the state and who adhered to fundamentalist Islam, as they were mostly graduates of al-Azhar Mosque-University. That rule also introduced the modern educational system, where the classrooms were made available for this kind of Islam to flourish. It took the whole period of this colonial rule for this particular battle to be fought out.

The Mahdia state (1885AD-1899AD) represents the ultimate victory of fundamentalist Islam over Sufi Islam. Muḥammad 'Abdullāhi the Mahdi himself was a Sufi man who revolted against what he perceived as leniency on the part of the Sufi sheikhs towards the pagan traditions of people which, according to his views, were not following the book of Sharīʿa. The Sufi amulet was thrown away, the fundamentalist robe put on. The Mahdia state understandably followed a strict fundamentalist Islam. Thereafter, Sufi Islam gradually identified with fundamentalist Islam so as to catch up in the long run. By the late decades of the 20th century the two could hardly be distinguished from each other. Both were in each case responsible for the two fanatical states in the second half of the 20th century, namely that of President Jaʿfar Nimeiri (1969-1985) and the present regime of President ʿUmar al-Bashīr (1989- up to the present).

The British-Egyptian colonial rule (1899AD-1956AD) resumed the same system of the Turco-Egyptian rule with regard to the government-sponsored education and the culture of official Muslim clergymen. By the time the Sudan achieved independence, the educated class was mostly orientated toward fundamentalist Islam. This showed in the rising tide of the Islamic fundamentalist movements among the students of higher educational institutions who followed the tenets of the Muslim Brotherhood, which was established by Ḥasan al-Banna in Egypt in 1928.

1.5.2. The Frustration of the Muslims

In the struggle of most of the Muslim nations for independence, the tide of the Islamic movements was not high enough to flood the shore. But they would excel themselves in mobilizing the people against the inept national governments that took over from the colonial ruler. The intelligentsia that formed those governments was the elite class that was expected to launch modernism in their traditional Islamic cultures. Superficially they ended up dressing and speaking like their colonial masters, but behaving like the local patriarchal despots - the only authority they knew of in their traditional society. Lacking any progressive vision pertaining to both their tradition, in which Islam is central, and to modernism, in which democracy is central, their rule was marked with corruption, dictatorship and shallow secularism that simply discarded religion out of ignorance. Thus they made themselves an easy target for the equally superficial Muslim fundamentalists.

The post-colonial Muslim societies hungered for progress, something that could only be achieved by taking stock of the whole system of values and thought. Neither their fake secular intellectuals nor their fanatical Islamic fundamentalists were equipped with any applicable vision for that. By the end of the 20th century, Muslims would be abused in the name of Caesar, as well as in the name of God. The Sudanese people had their fair share of this misfortune.

1.5.3. The Failure of Muslim Brothers

It took the Muslim Brothers of Sudan – under their spiritual leader Ḥasan al-Turābi – half a century of relentless activity and meticulous organization to assume power, through a coup d`etat that lacked public support to the extent that for a long time they could not admit that they were behind it. Propelled by the vigour of fanaticism, they immediately embarked on the sublime mission of reshaping the people according to what they believed was the right way ordained by God. As far as they were concerned, the people either expectantly or resignedly waited for the knowledge from on high to pour on them. But to the dismay of everybody – foe and friend alike – the Muslim Brothers have turned out after half a century of struggle to be poorly equipped for such a sublime mission. They were only equipped with a whip that they used to flog the people with.

Administratively they made favouritism, nepotism and preferential treatment the rule, and impartiality an exception that could only take place as a result of negligence. As if they were afraid this would be their last chance, they frantically and shamelessly began appropriating wealth from the public funds for education, health, food, housing etc. For the first time since the Turco-Egyptian colonial rule, the institution of the state was completely utilized against the benefit of the taxpayer with nothing spent on public services. This regime will indeed leave a lasting memory among the Sudanese people due to the blunders that cemented its place in historical records.

Faced by the truth that they had neither a vision nor a programme to follow for reshaping the people, and lulled by the swivel chairs of power, they either allowed themselves to lapse into laxity or were consumed by dissent. That was when their own time to be reshaped by the Sudanese culture began. At first they showed a self-conscious tolerance toward certain cultural aspects of Sudanese life such as singing, dancing, etc., which they had dismissed indignantly in the past. Eventually they began practising them. At present a considerable number of them have regained their senses and permanently abandoned fanaticism, but not by any means majority. Notwithstanding the shock of disillusion, the majority of Muslim Brothers has kept the tint of fundamentalism supported by a down to earth pragamatism. It may be argued that it is good that generally they have remained Islamist, because now it is hoped that they can develop into sensible, thoughtful Islamists instead of romantic fanatics.

It took the Muslim Brothers in the Sudan half a century (from circa 1940 to 1990) to learn this basic lesson of dealing with Islamic conceptual issues as matters pertaining to daily-life realism rather than retrospective idealism. Is it going to take a similarly long time for the other Islamic movements to learn this basic lesson (for example the *Anṣār al-Sunna al-Muḥammadiyya* "the Supporters of Muhammadan Traditions" who adhere to the strict *Wahhābi* fundamentalist orientation supported by the Kingdom of Saudi Arabia and who are considered to be even more fanatical than the Muslim Brothers), or will they prove to be wise enough to learn the lesson of their own accord? The important question is this: why should the Sudanese people become subjected to such arbitrary experiments with the entire blunder they centail? The cultural rehabilitation from religious fanaticism may prove to be much too expensive. They made their coup d'ētat in 1989 in order to prevent a peace initiative negotiated upon the premises of unity of Sudan from being endorsed by the democratically elected government, only to end up with a treaty that was based on the disintegration of the country which took place in 2011 (the secession of South Sudan). They began their rule with hostile slogans and chants directed against the superpowers of that time, the USA and the Soviet Union (both of them!), only to end up shamelessly eager to appease the USA to the extent of becoming a tool in the plot to break up the country into small sheikhdom states run by the USA.

1.5.4. Islam and the New World Order

Today in the 21st century, with America being the sole superpower, Islam has the potential to pose as a counterpower, unless Europe rises up to challenge America. Muslims all over the world harbour deep resentment towards the West in general and America in particular, for what truly seem to be double standards when dealing with issues that concern the Third World in general and the Muslim world in particular. In the event that Europe stands up to challenge America that may bring her closer to the Islamic world, in her search for an ally. That may relax the tension a little. The problem of the Islamic world is that it challenges America in a gangster-like or at best by employing guerrilla warfare. The Islamic think tank for such a huge battle is so little that fanaticism has come to look from outside as to be the driving force behind the fight against the West while it is really being manipulated by it. Bearing in mind its own experience in dealing with the Christian fanaticism of the Dark Ages, which was far worse than the Islamic fanaticism, the West is well prepared to win this battle. Superficially it may seem that out of vanity and for the sake of settling worthless accounts with Islam, certain strong circles of power and the mass media in the West prefer to have it this way, thus undermining any leading role the enlightened intellectuals of the Muslim world can play. However, the truth is that while Islamic fanaticism is locally engendered, it is being systematically manipulated by the West and used so as to weaken the infant nation states with a Muslim majority. Such fanatical movements as Boko Haram and the Islamic State (IS) could have never gained momentum without being supported by the West with regard to finance and logistics. To trick the Muslim public and make them look to their fanatical followers as facing and challenging the west, the fanatical movements are falsely propelled into an anti-western direction while their gun points are directed against their Muslim brethren's heads and chests. This practice of manipulating fanatical Islamic movements is very old; it goes back to the late 19th century up to the present (cf. Curtis, 2012; Josh Rogin, 14 June 2014, Double Dealing: America's Allies Are Funding ISIS, in:

http://www.thedailybeast.com/articles/2014/06/14/america-s-allies-are-funding-isis.html

It is true that if the Muslims are destined to develop and flourish, they have to achieve this goal while satisfying their conscience, which is inseparable from their belief. This has given us one of the caveats of the present-day that it is extremely difficult for any political movement to flourish among Muslims if it does not have its own Islamic discourse. To sideline Islam and ignore it will only give a boost to fanaticism, and fanaticism can effectively destroy, but it cannot construct. For any modern Islamic school of thought to be put forward, certain basic issues should be thoughtfully considered and then endorsed: democracy (not necessarily liberalism), human rights, and secularism. Only then can the battle with the West be won, not because these are the values of the West – a matter highly controversial, as the West seems to hate nothing more than to see these same values properly applied outside its frontiers – but rather because, generally speaking, the aesthetic values of democracy and human rights are to be referred to the oneness of human nature. There is no need to mention that the West is mostly responsible for toppling infant democratic governments all over the third world. Paradoxically, under the pretext of defending these values from being violated, the West also militarily intervenes in the third world countries and occupies them. The British-American invasion and the subsequent occupation of Iraq is an indication that occupational colonialism may resurface at any time, in full force. By doing exactly what Israel has been doing for the last 50 years regarding the occupation of other people's lands under the pretext of containing trouble, America and Britain have disqualified themselves as mediators of peace and campaigners for democracy. At present, with Donald Trump, a buffoon who is racist down to his morrow, becoming the president of the USA, occupational recolonialism of Africa has been flatly announced as a viable policy for the future.

In such an international context, post-modern Islam can come forward as one of the very progressive and anti-hegemonic and co-existent religions, along with Christianity and noble religions of Africa, South America and Asia.

1.6. Slavery

Slavery is a history-long human vice. It began by placing fighters captured in war times into compulsory work. Later it extended to abducting vulnerable people while they travelled or wandered alone or in small groups. Then it developed into organizing highly armed raids against peaceful human settlements in order to enslave free people either for work, military purposes, sex or all. Lastly, it became a State-policy vice, where first the Islamic empire and second the West were the chief culprits and Africa the main victim. All nations were involved in slavery and all the members of their respective societies were potentially subject to slavery.

1.6.1. The West and Slavery

Long before the Christianization of the Roman Empire, the institution of slavery in the West endorsed another human vice, namely racism. The Slavic people of Eastern Europe were targeted by slavery to the extent that every individual was assumed to be a slave. The word "slave" therefore exists in many European languages. However, that was secondary racism since difference in color was not yet an active factor of slavery. It was therefore cultural prejudice, since differences between the enslaver and the enslaved were in culture and language rather than in colour. Until this time slavery was not yet associated with blackness. The Moors, i.e. the ancient people of North Africa, were black just like the Pharaohs of ancient Egypt and Nubia, but that did not affect the high social status they held. It is also worth mentioning that the first two Roman viceroys in England were of black African origin.

In Judaism the sons of Ham, the latter erroneously taken to be the apical father of the blacks, were cursed by God (cf. the Bible, Genesis 9:25), hence they have come bearing African features (cf. Goldberg, 2003; Yamauchi, 2004). That is where Christianity took its own bias against blackness. Thus the Christianization of Europe paved the way for a culture of anti-blackness. From Rome and Byzantium it gradually moved westward to infect the whole of Europe. Until a certain Pope ordered that Jesus Christ be reproduced in the Raphaelian white man images, the paintings invariably revealed a dark-skinned Jesus. As Nubia was the corridor to black Africa, so we find in classical English dictionaries that the word "Nubian" collocates with "slave".

1.6.2. The Arabs and Slavery

By the time of the rise of the Arabs just before Islam, slavery had already taken root with a racial base grounded in colour, a factor that would prove to have a long-lasting effect. Henceforth, slavery would be increasingly associated with the colour black, thus making Africa the prime target. The infection of racial slavery came to Arabia from Judaism and Christianity.

The Arabs, a dark-skinned people themselves, began showing in their culture a strong orientation toward lighter skin. Their pre-Islamic and Islamic poetry is replete with racial and derogatory themes about the colour black. A famous pre-Islamic poet (ʿAntara bn. Shaddād), whose mother was a black African with fuzzy hair, painfully suffered from discrimination; his people did not recognize him even after he had proved his ultimate knighthood in tribal wars. The Prophet Muḥammad addressed this problem many times in his teachings. A close companion of his (Bilāl bn. Rabāḥ), who was a black of African origin, suffered a lot from colour-based derogatory remarks made by other Muslim brethren. Late in the Abbasid era, the blacks of Arabia led a revolt against discrimination. They plundered the cities they captured one after the other, and put everyone they chanced upon to the sword.

By the end of the Abbasid Caliphate the Arabic word for "black" had become synonymous with the word "slave", just as the word "nigger" became synonymous with "slave" in Western languages. However, enslaving white people did not stop. Slavery for hard labour was almost restricted to black Africans. Children from non-black communities, especially from the Caucasian regions in Central Asia, were abducted in order to be sold either for soldiery in the case of the males, or for the harem in the case of the females. Even so they were not called slaves. The former was called "*mamlūk*" (pl. *Mamālīk*), which literally means "owned", and the latter was called "*jāriya*", i.e. "mistress". They were exempted from the derogatory word "slave" simply because they were not black.

In Egypt those white slaves (or *al-Mamālīk*) managed to assume the rule of the country for almost 1000 years, only to be removed by Muḥammad ʿAli Pasha – himself an Albanian Ottoman mercenary – in the early 19th century. One of those mamlūk, however, was a black African called *Kāfūr al-Ikhshīdi*, who was thought by some scholars to have been enslaved from the Nuba Mountains in Sudan. He managed to usurp power from his master who was the governor and became the ruler of Egypt. "*Kāfūr*" was then a typical name for a black slave. In one of the most famous Arab derogatory poems made by the equally famous poet Al-Mutanabbi, he was bluntly called "*ʿabd*" i.e. slave, and further mocked by the advice that no slave should be bought without a stick to straighten them up with. (Ironically, for years this infamous piece of poetry was taught in Sudanese schools). Thus by the Middle Ages any black was subject to be called slave in the Arab and Islamic world.

Some African writers tried to argue in favour of Arab enslavement in comparison with Western enslavement of black Africans (cf. Mazrui, 2002). The strong argument of Mazrui goes as follows: the evident existence of black Africans in America today (in tens of millions) compared to the unnoticed existence of them in Arabia (in tens of thousands); the huge number of slaves who perished while being transported across the Atlantic compared with the relatively small number on the other side due to the proximity of Africa to Arabia. While we may fully agree with this argument, there exist a couple of major factors that have contributed greatly to the degradation of black Africans in the Arabia of yesterday and of today, and they have failed to merit the attention of Mazrui. One of them is the fact that the proximity of colour between the Africans and the Arabs might have absorbed the difference. Another is the fact that while very few of the trans-Atlantic slaves succeeded in returning home, a considerable number of African slaves did manage to return to Africa from Arabia. There is also the population factor in comparison between America (huge) and Arabia (small). The main counter-argument to that of Mazrui, however, is that in Arabia the culture of slavery still thrives and is explicit in fact that a free black person is usually dubbed as slave (cf. Prah, 2006a). In comparison, the anti-black sentiments in America and the West in general are controlled and illicit (*ibid*). Last but not least, in Arabia, we are centuries away from an Obama phenomenon, if it will ever be possible.

1.6.3. The Reinstatement of Slavery Auctions in Libya

In November 2017, the world awoke to the shocking news coming from Libya showing how black African migrants coming to Libya to cross the Mediterranean to Europe were being sold as slaves in open auctions. This news, however, was not new; it was known for almost four years before that by millions of black Africans who were crying in the wilderness of the 21st century globalization era but to no avail, while following the horrendous sufferings of their brethren who were being sold and bought by the Arabs in Libya while the European Union watching it silently.

The Arabs, generally speaking and up to the present, live with the mind-set of the slavers of yesterday. This means that they remain potential enslavers whenever and wherever they chance the favourable conditions and the unlucky wretched people. Egypt's Minister for the Environment and President of the African Ministerial Conference on the Environment (AMCEN) is said to have referred to his Sub-Saharan African colleagues as "dogs and slaves" during a debate as the United Nations Environment Assembly (UNEA-2) came to a close on Friday May 27, 2016, simply because a resolution on Gaza was not adopted due to a lack of a quorum (https://tuko.co.ke/134967-drama-un-nairobi-egypt-minister-calls-africans-dogs-slaves.html). If this is how Arabs at the top think of Sub-Saharan Africans, the ordinary Arabs are even worse.

Under the circumstances of state collapse in Libya and absence of both capable central government and law, and the keen efforts of the European Union (EU) to curb the trans-Saharan, trans-Mediterranean emigration at any cost, the rein has been not only intentionally loosened by the EU for a couple of states in Africa to help discourage black Africans from thinking of taking the deadly adventure of crossing the Mediterranean to Europe via Libya, but further the EU agreed to finance and help the Islamo-Arabist regime of Khartoum in logistics to close its borders with Libya. The government of Sudan (GoS) took the money and brought in the infamous *Janjawīd* militias, which are extorting money from the border crossers. Any crosser who fails to pay would be shot dead on the head. Later who had paid would be handed to the human-trafficking gangsters- just as that!

According to *the Sunday Express* (May 15 2016), documents relating to the EU project in Africa suggest Europe has reached a deal with the regime of the Sudanese to help in curbing the flow of emigrants across Sudan's border has been settled upon which the Sudan will police the borders and the EU will assist with the necessary fund and logistics for camps and detention rooms (for more details, see: http://www.express.co.uk/news/world/670550/EU-secret-deal-war-criminal-Sudan-migrant-crisis-Africa). This shows how the EU is ready to broker deals with a criminal regime presided over by a criminal president. Not only that concerns over how the equipment could be used by Sudan's criminal regime had been expressed, but further reports by the human rights groups accused the Sudanese police and military of selling the refugees to human traffickers (Patrick Kingsley. 2018).

The government of the Sudan (GoS) was more keen to appease the EU than to curb the trans-Saharan emigration. It simply handed the money and logistics provided by the EU to the infamous *Janjawīd* militias which are mostly formed from the Bedouin Arabs of Chad, Niger, Mali, and Nigeria, and who have been marauding Darfur for so many years, killing indigenous black Africans, systematically raping the women, torching up the villages, and eventually displacing the indigenous people of Darfur with no less than half a million dead so far, while the Darfur saga is still going on. Now almost all the deserted villages have been repopulated by Arab tribes from the above named countries in the biggest demographic engineering policy in the 21st century so far.

The measure the *Janjawīd*'s Arab militias took after stationing themselves at the border crossing points was simply taking as hostages all border-crossers who cut across various nationalities such as Sudanese, Eritrean, Ethiopian, South Sudanese etc. The *Janajwīd* militias literally sold them to Libyan agents who resold them to other Libyans who were in need of free labour. This has been going on like that for the last two to three years. All those participants (Europeans and Arabs alike) have something in common: the mind-set of the enslaver with its historical stereotype that any black African is a potential slave.

Right from the beginning of the reinstatement of slavery in Libya, the EU, American authorities along with their complicit human rights organizations and mass media companies were fully aware of what was going on there. They intentionally turned a blind eye to it until it built into a full scale slavery institution. Their plan was that the worldwide media exposure of the open-auction slavery would hopefully have enough impact on black Africans not to think of coming to Libya to work there, let alone to think of going there to cross the Mediterranean into Europe. And now they believe that it has achieved its objectives. That is when they decided to expose it!

However, in the age of globalization, on can hardly deceive the world. The truth will very soon surface. Amnesty International (2017) has pointed the finger of accusation at the European governments, accusing them of being complicit in the torture and abuse of migrants and refugees in Libya. However, Amnesty International decided to give its report the title of (Libya's Dark Web of Collusion: Abuses Against Europe-bound Refugees and Migrants); it was just one step from using the word "black" instead of "dark", disclosing the same mind-set of enslavers that has propelled Europe in the first place to enslave the Africans and this time Libya to become only complicit. In this it is not less complicit than the EU. In this time of aggregate mass media, nothing is easier than obliterating the truth by heaping on its head a torrential flow of news of different kind, unless there is serious follow-up.

Under the banner: People for sale: exposing migrant slave auctions in Libya (https://edition.cnn.com/specials/africa/libya-slave-auctions), the CNN began showing its reportage of the human auctions in Libya, but not without the cooperation of the faltering Libyan government. No Arab or African country, generally speaking, will open up all its gates (including prisons and concentration camps) to allow such damaging TV reportage. In these parts of the world, no TV reportage, which is extremely revealing and damaging, can be done in the open, with government officials helping and willing to give positive statements rather than being in total denial. This shows how the CNN is part of the international complicity at the very moment when it is boasting of doing this for the sake of the truth.

While condemning the faltering Libyan government, we must not be naive and forget about the other actors such as the Sudanese Islamo-Arab government and its *Janjawīd* Arab militias who initiated this in the first place. Along with this, we must not let the mastermind of all this get away with it that is the EU, UK, and USA in particular and their puppet human rights organizations and poodling mass media companies. They seem to have not only come to this renewed vice of slavery with experience that kept accumulating over the centuries, but also with a long suppressed appetite.

1.6.4. The Western Mass Enslavement of Africans

With the coming of the age of geographical explorations and industrialization, the West frantically stormed Africa from all directions in pursuit of slaves, and in the process displaying evilness that is unprecedented in the history of mankind. Populous Africa was depopulated in a few decades. When slavery was abandoned, it was a matter of achieving equilibrium in means and modes of production – paid-labour production could not compete with unpaid-slave-labour production. The ethical value of human freedom was just exploited in the same way that the helpless slave was. After all, it was Abraham Lincoln, the 16th President of the USA and the so-called slave liberator, who said: "I will say, then, that I am not, nor ever have been, in favour of bringing about in any way the social and political equality of the white and black races [applause]: that I am not, nor ever have been, in favour of making voters or jurors of negroes, nor of qualifying them to hold office, nor to intermarry with white people; and I will say in addition to this that there is a physical difference between the white and black races which I believe will forever forbid the two races living together on terms of social and political equality. And inasmuch as they cannot so live, while they do remain together there must be the position of superior and inferior, and I as much as any other man am in favour of having the superior position assigned to the white race" (September 18, 1858, in a speech in Charleston, Illinois; cf. Lincoln-Douglas debates, 1858: www.founding.com).

Africa has come out of this with an eternal wound, the West with eternal shame. To add to its historical shame, the West, generally speaking, has not shown any remorse or at least thankfulness for the blacks who died while toiling and tilling the land for their masters, let alone reparation. For instance, the British monarchy has persistently refused to apologize for slavery. The West all through the 20th century tolerated apartheid, which is the legitimate child of the marriage of slavery and racism. In fact, the degeneracy and degradation, which was the impetus for the institution of slavery, survived up to the present to serve as a psychological catalyst for neo-colonialism and imperialism. This is how the people of the Third World are being badly treated by the governments of the First World: manipulation, exploitative intervention and double standards. In particular, they are taking black Africans lightly because deep down in their psyche, the contention of degeneracy still survives.

1.6.5. *Al-Jallāba* of Sudan: the Slave Procurers

Slavery was practised in Sudan from ancient times. The Muslim Arabs in the Paqt treaty (642AD) between them and the Nubian Christian kingdom of Nobatia (in an area presently straddling the Sudan-Egypt border) demanded in return for wheat and vintage wine etc, to annually receive, among other things, 360 slaves who were brought from the hinterlands. The slaves were not yet a cash commodity, nor were they wage-free labour in a capitalist system, as would develop into a little later. Although it can be argued that traditional African slavery resulting from petty tribal feuds and wars was still the main source of slaves, to have that annually-paid number of slaves as a retail commodity embedded in an international treaty poses a host of questions pertaining to the geographical areas and ethnic entities that were targeted by the Nubians to fulfill that condition. The effects of the slave condition are far deeper in Sudanese society than contemporary historians have considered.

It is believed by the present writer that the tendency to simply call the people of the peripheries 'slaves' in present day Sudan can be traced back to the Paqt Treaty of 642AD. The coming of the 16th century witnessed the end of the last Nubian kingdom in the Sudan and also the official end of Christianity. In 1505AD the era of the Islamic and Arabic kingdom of the Funj (the Black Sultanate, 1505AD - 1821AD) began. Slavery continued to be practised as a collateral result of civil wars all through the time of the Funj Sultanate until the Europeans began making incursions into the continent to procure slaves.

It was the Turco-Egyptian colonial rule (821AD - 1885AD) that launched the era of mass slavery in the Sudan. They made it a state-policy loaded with the whole weight of the Arab ideological stigmatization of the blacks. Locally, the Arabized people of middle and northern Sudan, whose ideological centre was growing fast, imitated them. They played the role of the intermediary who organized the raids, captured the blacks and then sold them. The term *al-Jallāba* is a plural adjective in Sudanese colloquial Arabic literally meaning the procurers. The singular is *al-Jallābi*. The term originated in reference to the intermediary slavers who were mostly Arabized Sudanese. The culture of *al-Jallāba* had a big impact in consolidating the establishment of the centre. When the Turco-Egyptian colonial rule was compelled to abolish slavery, *al-Jallāba* defied that and boldly continued to practise it. By that time they had developed their raiding squads into formidable armies. As their top slaver (al-Zubayr wad Raḥama) forced his way in and became governor of some parts of Baḥar al-Ghazāl and Darfur, they were just one step away from taking over the rule of the country. When his de facto governorship was recognized, the prestigious title of "Pasha" was bestowed on him. The *Jallābas* cherished the prospect of inheriting the faltering Turco-Egyptian rule. If it were not for the Mahdia revolution that might have taken place. The Mahdia State (1885AD - 1899AD), strictly following the scriptures of Islam, where there is no direct verse from either the Qur'ān or the Prophet's traditions abolishing slavery, indulged itself in reinstating the institution of slavery. However, it strongly abolished tobacco and snuff whether chewed or smoked, although there is also no direct verse either from the Qur'ān or the Prophet's traditions to that effect. Understandably the pragmatic and Machiavellian *Jallābas* were among the first to declare their allegiance to the Mahdia. They put their huge military resources and expertise at the service of the revolution. That is one of the reasons why the Mahdia State came to belong ideologically to the Islamo-Arab centre.

Backed by its colonialist pragmatism, the British-Egyptian colonial rule (1899AD - 1956AD) very soon consolidated its alliance with the Islamo-Arab centre. Although officially declared abolished, slavery was tolerated as a practice and culture (cf. Sikainga, 1996). It was not in the interest of either the British or the Egyptians to enlighten, for instance, the Sudanese youngsters in schools about the vices of slavery or the fallacy of associating it with a certain colour, particularly blackness, as it is the colour of the whole Sudanese people. To both the British and Egyptians all Sudanese people were blacks. Such an approach could have shaken the stability of the Islamo-Arab centre, thus threatening the colonial rule itself.

The post-colonial national government clearly showed its stance in this regard by naming a street in Khartoum after al-Zubayr Pasha, the most notorious slaver in Sudan's modern history. To tell the truth, the culture of slavery was behind the bad treatment of the Southerners by the successive national governments that took place under the pretext of curbing the civil war. Civil war will always give vent for the culture of slavery to tacitly express itself.

1.7. Silencing Sudanese Music by an Inconvenient Ideology

Below we are going to indulge in a panoramic sweep through the last one and a half millennium attempting to trace the musical genres of the Sudan as being African in origin and tracing how the process of Islamization and Arabization has affected them. The advent of Christianity can roughly be said to have begun around the 6th century AD. The processes of Islamization and Arabization can also be marked with the establishment of the Black Sultanate of the Funj in 1505 AD.

Like any African society, the Sudanese communities in pre-Arab Sudan had their musical performances, in which the following can be concluded: 1) drums, i.e. rhythm; 2) dancing, whether rituals or for casual entertainment; 3) musical instruments; 4) lyrics; and 5) the mixing of males and females with no gender segregation. The most common musical instruments are those of the string (such as the lyre), wind (such as the horns) and drum (such as '*dallūka*'), as they are found in almost all the regions of Sudan (al-Ḍaw, 1985).

1.7.1. Music in Pre-Arab Sudanese Communities

Let us now review the African characteristics of the Sudanese music among African ethnic groups. The various genres and instruments will also be reviewed. In doing this, we will pinpoint the Islamo-Arab ideological tangles that it eventually found itself involved in.

1.7.1.1. Music in Western Sudan

Al-Tūnusi (1965: 231-241), who visited Darfur in the first decade of the 19th century, tells us how women and men sang and danced at the royal court, with most of them under the effect of alcohol. He further gives a list of the dances in the region. He gives a detailed description of the '*shikindira*' dance, which is still one of the well-known dances of Darfur today. In this dance, the girls and boys will form a circle with the former stooping forward touching the ground with their hands. The boys will come at the back of the girls holding them firmly from the waist.

Such genres have come under threat as a result of Islamization ('Abduljalīl & Khāṭir, 1977: 101). The new surge of Islamic puritans and fundamentalists began in the mid-20th century. Organized groups of fundamentalist Muslims took to moving from town to town and from village to village, preaching a strict version of Islam that does not condone of any feature of creative entertainment such as music, singing and dancing.

7.1.1.2. Music in Eastern Sudan

The historical people of Eastern Sudan, i.e. the Beja, usually represent this region, though many ethnic groups populate it. More than one scholar has mentioned that nothing is easier for the Beja person than to start singing (cf. Sanders, 1935: 214; Newbold, 1936: 140-141; Clark, 1938: 5). Ohaj, a Beja historian himself, mentions that the Beja perform in a group using the lyre to sing and dance (Ohaj, 1986: 13-17). Ibrahim (1991) also mentions that each Beja clan has its own tunes defining their each ethnic-boundary (*agāyēb*). This tune should only be played for declaring war. No one outside the clan is allowed to play this tune unless they want to announce their presence within the precinct of the clan. In this case, food and drinks will be offered to the guests to urge them to stop playing the tunes. If they keep playing it, then this will be taken as an insult to the tribe and it may lead the tribesmen to kill immediately the guest (Ibrahim, 1991).

1.7.1.3. The Music in Southern Sudan

The travelers and government officials in the time of both Turco-Egyptian rule (1821-1885) and the Condominium rule (1899–1956) recorded many aspects of music among southern Sudanese communities. Schweinfurth (1874: 413-445) tells of a performance done by Monza, king of the Nyam-Nyam tribes in Equatoria. Wyndham (1937) tells of the folkloric and musical genres of the Baria, Azandi, Nuer and Dinka. In fact, music and dancing play a central role in the rites of passage and life circle in almost all the tribes of southern Sudan (cf. Leinhardt, 1961).

1.7.1.4. The Music in Northern Sudan

The Nubians can be taken as representing the North, having been indigenous to the region for thousands of years. The region houses other tribes, such as the great Ja'aliyyin tribes; however, the link between them and the Nubians is very strong, bearing in mind the opinion that classifies them as Arabized Nubians (cf. Fadl, 1973: 145-154). The Nubians have their various musical folkloric genres. These varieties go according to the inter-ethnic differentiations, such as The Dongula in the upper region; Maḥas, Sukkoud, and Ḥalfa down the river (cf. Simon, 1980a). As they were Christians until a few centuries ago (Vantini, 1981), with music being part of their religious practices, it is to be expected that music has played a central role in their cosmology. In fact we know of some of the hymns they used to perform during the time of Christianity (cf. Griffith, 1913; Browne, 1989). Burckhardt (1978) who visited the region in 1813-14 mentions that the lyre was the only instrument he came across among the Nubians. Waddington & Hanbury (1822: 250), who visited the region with the invading Turco-Egyptian army, tell us about their encounter with the kings of the Maḥas. They tell in particular about the royal bards in both the Nubian kingdoms of Maḥas and Argo and the crucial role played by them. In this regard, it is worth mentioning that they fit into the type and style of the royal bards in other areas of Africa (cf. Mafaje, 1961). It is interesting that Lepsius (1880: 240) includes one of the songs performed for him by a Maḥas royal bard. In 2001 the present writer, when doing field research among the Maḥas, succeeded in identifying the same song still being performed at Kukke (the village seat of the Maḥas kingdom). Further evidence of the African origin of the musical genres and performances of the Nubians is in the book by Musul (1974) where he cites all forms of dances, songs and musical instruments in the Sukkout region in middle Sudanese Nubia.

1.7.2. The Music in Middle Islamized and Arabized Sudan

Next we turn to the other side to see the music right in the milieu of the Islamo-Arab ideology. The first thing that is going to strike us is the simple fact that singing, generally speaking, is flatly forbidden, but not without exceptions. What is most striking is the fact that the main exception applies to the class of slaves.

1.7.2.1. The Funj Era (1505 - 1820)

Middle Sudan is usually represented by the Arabised and Islamized Africans (cf. Fadl, 1973). The Funj sultanate, also called 'the Black Sultanate', was allegedly the first Islamic and Arab kingdom to have command of the middle region and other peripheral areas such as Kordufan, the east and the north. In the Arab-Islamic era people were discouraged from performing music unless it was to praise Prophet Muhammad; music performers were given the derogatory name '*al-ṣuyyā'*', the plural of '*ṣāyi*', i.e. vagabond (al-Tahir, 1993). In their Prophet-praising chants, the Sufi bands employed the drums and brass percussion (cf. Simon, 1980b). However, there was a certain Sufi shaikh (Isma'il al-Daglāshi) who used to play music with the '*rabbāba*' (the lyre) until he was nicknamed 'Ismā'īl the one with the *rabbāba*'. In his songs, which were a mixture of Sufism and flirtation, he used to allude to specific known women, a matter that caused him trouble (see his biography in Wad Ḍaif Allah, 1985). Girls of noble tribal origin, i.e. of Arabized tribes, were allowed only to sing in order to incite their people to go to war, or to mourn their dead, a brother, a father or son. Singing, in the way known to us now, was left to their slaves.

1.7.2.2. The Turco-Egyptian Era (1821 - 1885)

Among other secondary objectives, the Turco-Egyptian government in Egypt invaded the Sudan primarily to acquire gold and procure slaves. Muhammad Ali Pasha needed the gold to build his newly-born empire; he needed the slaves to recruit them into the army to protect his empire. The areas targeted with the slavery raids were the South, Nuba Mountains, Funj, Hamaj, Ingassan (upper Blue Nile) and Darfur (Ibrahim, 1971: 5-22). Those enslaved soldiers were put into battalions according to their ethnic backgrounds, i.e. those of Dinka origin would form their own regiment and so on (cf. Mohamed, 1980: 15-16). Music and vocal performances in the middle of the Sudan were not touched by the new rule as it left it in its old tradition of discouraging them in preference to the praising of Prophet Muhammad and the Sufi saints.

By the mid-19th century, the urban areas began growing fast, with the class of ex-slave soldiers forming a community in its own right. This community, mostly or completely detribalized (a term, first coined by Kurita, 1997, used here with great reservation), was different in so many ways from the fully tribalized classes of middle Sudan. The membership of that detribalized community was considered by the tribalistically prestigious communities as a social stigma. However, the more the government and the communities of middle Sudan indulged themselves in slavery, the more the detribalized people kept growing as an urban community with clearly liberal tendencies. In 1851 James Hamilton, an English traveler, relates how he was entertained in Khartoum with a party where beautiful, young girls danced while veiled women sat at the back (1857: 323-328).

By then, the Nubians of northern Sudan, particularly the Maḥas, had based themselves in and around Khartoum. They were the pioneers of Sufi sects in the era of Islam and Arabization. Coming from an African background, with Arabization as the only way to prosper, they maintained a balance between adhering to the tradition of performing music only to praise the prophet and for the sake of entertainment. The sons and descendants of their renowned Sufi families began performing flirtacious music in their youth to resort to Sufi chants when they got older. The most famous for this kind is Shaikh Mudawwi, the great-grandson of the *Maḥasi* Ṣufi Shaikh Idrīs wad al-Arbāb. Shaikh Muḍawwi began by composing some of the fine songs that are still being performed. Later, when he became older, he went to the *ḥajj* (pilgrimage) and thenceforth concentrated on Ṣufi chants and religion; eventually he was chosen as head of his family Ṣufi sect.

The slave-based regiments and battalions kept playing their own ethnic music, which was modified to serve as military marches. These songs and chants were the composite of present day marches of the Sudanese military, with the lyrics of most of them being well known

(Jabir, n.d.). When the Turco-Egyptian regime was compelled to abandon slavery, it began recruiting soldiers with the consent of the tribal leaders in the same areas that were subject to slave raids. In 1858, on his visit to the Sudan, the khedive of Egypt Sa'īd Pasha gave orders to form a military musical band by recruiting youngsters from certain black tribes. Among those who were recruited was Abdullah ʿAdlān who was the son of the chief of the Funj tribe (Bredin, 1961: 37-45). Later, the Yuzbashi Abdullah ʿAdlān became the first maestro of the military band. In 1888, the British government, departing from Egypt, began reorganizing the army in order to invade the Sudan and occupy it by defeating the Mahdia army. As part of this, they began also reorganizing the so-called Sudanese battalions, which were made up of soldiers of ex-slave backgrounds. Later in 1930s, the Condominium Rule (1899 - 1956) developed them into what came to be known as the 'Sudan Defence Force' (Awad, 1978). Eventually the military band developed into the Musical Corps after independence in 1956.

1.7.2.3. The Mahdia Era (1885 - 1899)

Strictly following a fundamentalist religious legal system, the Mahdia immediately abolished music and singing (Slatin, 1898: 233). It particularly targeted the female dancers and performers, whom were flogged if caught singing (Fawzi, 1901: 170). This led to the silencing of many female performers who only came back to singing after the defeat of the Mahdia rule; among those was the famous Sharīfa bit Bilāl (al-Tahir, 1993: 25). The only genre of music allowed to men at that time was the '*karīr*' or '*ṭambūr*' (it has nothing to do with the musical instrument called '*ṭanbūr*'), which is a coarse oral music made by harshly blowing glottal sound from the throat. This is an old Sudanese musical genre that signifies virility and fertility and is usually performed by a group of men circling around girls and women who dance and sing.

1.7.2.4. The Colonial Condominium Era (1899 - 1956)

When the embargo on performing music was lifted by the end of the Mahdia, people began reviving their suppressed musical genres starting from where they were, i.e. the '*ṭambūr*'. At that time the urban class formed by the completely detribalized communities of ex-slave background was spared the trauma of the Mahdia as they had fled to Egypt only to come back with the invading army. Therefore, there were two parts of the society: (1) a self-suppressed part (Islamo-Arabized and fully tribalized people of middle Sudan who do not classify themselves as blacks), and (2) a self-liberated part who consisted of the detribalized blacks who bore the stigma of slavery. The paradox was that the latter were at greater advantage simply by the way they were (cf. Kurita, 1997). The detribalized blacks maintained their old genres of music and performances, which were enriched by the relatively academic excellence attained by the military band in which some of them participated. The two parts were in fact performing completely different genres of music.

1.7.3. Conclusion

A little later, the self-suppressed part began catching up with the old traditions of musical performance, which were enriched by the academic improvement referred to above in addition to the music and performances coming from the African tribes, i.e. the the historical source of slaves, now represented mostly in ex-slave descendents. The self-suppressed part began slowly merging artistically with the non-suppressed group giving us the so-called *ḥaqība* genre of song of modern riverain Sudan.

CHAPTER 2

The Arabization of the Sudan

2.1. The Scramble for Arab Genealogies

With the weakening of the Christian kingdoms, between the 14th and 16th centuries, new Islamic and Arabized small kingdoms (Shaikhdoms) began appearing and eventually succeeded in replacing the old regime (Yusuf Fadl, 1973; Shibeika, 1991). The first was the Kunūz (*Banī al-Kanz*) kingdom around the Asuan area in present-day Egyptian Nubia, to be followed a little later by the Rabīʿa-Beja Islamic kingdom of Hajar in northeastern Sudan. In the late 15th century the Islamic kingdom of Tegali (Togole) in the Nuba Mountains came into existence. A century later the Ottoman Sultan, Selim the Second, made a thrust deep into Nubia, in the aftermath of which appeared the Northern Nubian Islamic kingdoms of the Kushshāf, Maḥas, and Argo. Two centuries later the Fur kingdom of Keira was established upon the fall of the Tunjur kingdom. However the most important was the Funj sultanate, which came into existence in the early 16th century and which succeeded in spreading its influence over most of these small kingdoms. Many tribes in Southern Sudan began adopting some of the traits as a result of being exposed to this new wave of governance culture. In fact the unification of such small kingdoms along with many other tribal sheikhdoms is what has constituted the state in the ancient and present-day two Sudans.

The Funj sultanate came into existence with slavery looming in the background and with the black colour fully stigmatized by being synonymous with "slave". By the turn of the 15th century, Soba, the capital of the last Christian kingdom of Alodia, fell at the hands of the Arabized Nubians (pseudo-Arabs who claim to be Arab in the Sudan) led by ʿAbdu Allah Jammāʿ al-Girēnāti (*'Jammāʿ'*, an adjective literally meaning the "gatherer" for unifying the divided Arabs [*ʿArab al-Gawāsma*]; *'Girēnāti'*, a diminutive adjective literally meaning 'of the horns' in reference to the royal horned headgear as was the case in the Christian Kingdoms).

Immediately after the fall of Soba, a black African people called the Funj – led by ʿAmāra Dungus – appeared; he managed to settle a treaty with the self-styled Arabs after defeating them, in the process establishing the Funj sultanate. As the founders of it were virtually blacks, it was understandably called by its founders *'al-ṣalṭa al-zarga'*, i.e. the "Black sultanate". As it came in response to the growing influence of the Islamo-Arabized Nubians (the pseudo-Arabs), it explicitly showed an Arab and Islamic orientation. The new formations of Arabized tribes began claiming Arab descent supported by traditionally faked genealogies. The transformation from African identity to Arab identity is reflected in the ideological cliché of dropping the "matrilineal system", where only descent through the mother's lineage is recognized, and adopting the "patrilineal system", where only descent through the father's lineage is considered. The small family units compensated for their vulnerability by claiming the noble "*sharīf*" descent, i.e. descendants of Prophet Muḥammad. Eventually in the name of this descent they would appropriate both wealth and power, something the immediate descendants of the Prophet were not authorized to have while Muḥammad was still alive.

In order to be on an equal footing with these tribes in matters pertaining to power and authority, the Funj also claimed an Umayyad descent (the First Islamic Dynasty). Furthermore scholars in Arabic and Islamic sciences from other parts of the Islamic world were encouraged to settle in the Sudan.

This shows how Arab genealogies and identifying with Arab identity have come to play crucial roles in the power relations in the Sudan; hence, the power ideology of Islamo-Arabism. This ideological machinery of alienation has been working for the last five centuries. Over this course of time, this ideology has incurred the demise of the Sudan. Along with this, it will certainly bring about the demise of the borderland countries that border Arabia of North Africa on one side and Black Africa on the other side. These lands stretch from the Red Sea to the Atlantic Ocean of which Sudan is the model.

2.1.1. The Paradox of the Black Pseudo-Arab who is Anti-Black

Henceforth, the Arabized Africans of middle Sudan posed as non-black Arabs. Intermarriage with light-skinned people was consciously sought as a process of cleansing blood from blackness. A long process of identity change had begun. In order to have access to power and to be accepted as free humans at least, African people tended to drop both their identities and languages and replace them with Arabic language and identities. The first step to playing the game was to overtly deplore the blacks and dub them as slaves (while being themselves black). A new ideological awareness of race and colour came into being. The shades of the colour of blackness were perceived as authentic racial differentiations (cf. Deng, 1995). A Sudanese criterion for racial colour was formed by which the light black was seen as an Arab, "*wad 'Arab*" (descendant of Arabs) and "*wad balad*" (descendant of the country) [sic], both alluding to white or at least non-black. The jet-black Sudanese was seen as an African, i.e. slave (*'abd*). The shades of blackness go as follows, starting from jet-black (*aswad*): black (*azrag*, literally blue), brownish-black (*akhdar*, literally green), light-brownish (*gamḥi*, i.e. wheat-coloured), then dark-white, which is considered as white proper; this sub-category is paradoxically stigmatized more than the jet-black. Then a host of derogatory terms have been generated in the culture and colloquial Arabic of Middle Sudan, which dehumanize the black Africans, such as "*farikh*" (literally 'chick', here black one in particular), "*gargūr*" (a kind of Nile fish detested for living in mud), etc. In this context the properly white and light coloured, as mentioned above, are also discredited; they are given the derogatory name of "*ḥalab*" i.e. gypsy. A Sudanese Arab proverb says that "the slaves (i.e. black people) are second class, but the *ḥalab*s are third class."

2.2. Stigma vs. Prestigma

At that point in time, the seeds of the Sudanese ideology of Arab-oriented domination over Africans were sown. It works through two mechanisms: firstly, the stigma of slavery, blackness and people of African identity who occupy the margin of social and cultural status overlapped with the fact that their respective geographies surround the middle of the country where this ideology of hegemony has consolidated itself. Second, the prestigma (coined by the present writer from 'prestige' to serve as a counteracting term to stigma) of the free, non-black and

Arabs, who occupy the centre of power and culture, also overlapped with the fact that it is situated in the middle of the country. While the 'stigma' carries negative connotations, and the stigmatized people are abhorred, the 'prestigma' inversely has positive connotations and the prestigmatized people are admired and aspired to. This self-defeating ideology, in its drive to achieve self-actualization, underlines a process of alienation and subordination; these are black African people who do not recognize themselves as such. While posing as whites, they do not hold white people proper in high esteem. They tend to savagely dominate their fellow Africans by enslaving and stigmatizing them before largely indulging themselves in prestigmatizing the Arabs proper with whom they identify.

This ideology of alienation has prevailed for the past five centuries up to the present day. It has been consolidated by the successive political regimes whether Turco-Egyptian or Egyptian-British or national rule. It finds its roots in the vice of slavery. Therefore, it is no wonder that slavery was once again in full swing by the late 20th and early 21st centuries as a result of the state's extremely intensified processes of prestigmatic Islamo-Arabism. By sublimating the Arab as a model for themselves through this erroneously confused concept of race, the Arabized people of Sudan (pseudo-Arabs) have made themselves second-class Arabs. The repercussions of this will not only affect them, but their whole country, which will be split up between Arabism and Africanism. It has never dawned on them that speaking a language does not necessarily presuppose adopting the basic nationality engendering that language. In fact, the so-called Arab nation comprises different peoples with different cultures but one language; they are Arabophone. The Sudanese people are Arabophone Africans, just as there are Francophone and Anglophone Africans.

2.2.1. A Belated Self-Discovery?

The weak fabric of this colour concept was torn into tatters when the Sudanese prestigma came in contact with the Arabs proper in the mid-1970s, when they worked as expatriates in the rich petroleum states of Arabia. There, in the historical milieu of this racial bigotry, they amounted to nothing more than black Africans, i.e. slaves. It caused a turmoil that triggered a slow process of self-discovery, resulting in the weakening of the ideology of domination. By the mid-1990s, the image of the rebel leader of SPLM/SPLA, John Garang, who was a jet-black African from Southern Sudan, was much more acceptable to a great number of the Arabized Sudanese as the real leader of the whole movement of the political opposition to the Islamic regime of Khartoum. The military weight of SPLM/SPLA would never have mattered in making that acceptance possible if the ideology of domination had been still intact.

2.3. The Centro-marginalization Conflict

In the following paragraphs, the words "periphery" and "middle" are used only to refer to the geographical connotations. The words "centre" and "margin" are of purely ideological meaning referring to the Islamo-Arab ideology of hegemony of the pseudo-Arabs of the Sudan. Although roughly situated in the middle of Sudan, (if considered in terms of urbanization) the centre is neither restricted to geography nor to ethnicity or culture (cf. Hāshim, 2014). Rather, it is a centre of both power and wealth. Likewise, the margin is neither geographical nor ethnic or cultural; rather it is a margin with regard to power and wealth. With Islamo-Arabism as its main ideology, the centre poses as representing the interests of the Arabized people of middle Sudan; a notion erroneously believed by many sectors. It may be true that people from the centre mostly live in the peripheries and are always encouraged and tempted to join the centre by renouncing their African identities, cultures and languages and becoming Arabized. This complex process is made to look like a natural cultural interaction that takes place out of the necessity of leaving one's home village and coming to live in a town dominated by Arabs. This accounts for the confusion that the centre is more or less geographically situated while the margin refers also to the geographically peripheral area. Nothing can be more wrong (*ibid*).

The centre is very complex. In essence it is neither racial nor cultural nor geographical, neither Islamic nor Arab. Usually the spearheads of the centre are people who originally belonged to the margin, but have been lured through the educational system to alienate themselves from their people in order to appropriate wealth and power. Those should neither be counted as belonging to the margin, nor as representing their marginalized people. Within the Arabized people of middle Sudan itself there are different circular castes. As the centre is basically made up of Arabized Africans, a racially proper Arab would not merit any prestige. This is how the purely Arab tribe of Rashāyda of the Red Sea region has become marginalized to the extent of taking to arms against the state of the centre (*ibid*).

The centre in particular is rather the class of elites that has resulted from the non-developmental educational system, which was founded by the Turco-Egyptian rule that turns the smart pupils and students all through the educational system into self-centered parasites who suck the blood of the country while producing nothing. This educational system along with the elites it produced was designed by the Turco-Egyptian and British-Egyptian colonial regimes of yesterday when it sought to fill the petty governmental posts with nationals rather than foreigners from abroad. This is how education was designed to serve the colonial rule, not to fulfill the need of the society with regards to leadership and technical advancement. As the governmental institutions have always been stationed in urban areas, the educationally produced elites, who mostly came from very poor areas (the peripheries), did not have any place in their tiny villages. They had to move to where the governmental posts reside, i.e. the urban areas, not only to eventually alienate themselves from their villages and their poor people, but to serve the colonial rulers and imitate them in everything, clothes, behaviour and thinking. This class of the educationally produced elites achieves its own glory and splendor through the riches [*sic*] made available by governmental posts. Being a non-productive class, it tends to put all the resources of the government at its disposal. This class may look like originating in the pseudo-Arab middle of the Sudan, but this is false. It only appears to be so due to the simple fact that the state historically has resided in this Riverain middle of the country. At the commencement of independence, the colonial powers found no one there to pass the power to except this class. That was the real demise of the modern Sudan (*ibid*).

This centre of power and wealth makes use of all features of life, such as culture, race, history, especially Islam and Arabism. This centre of power and wealth processes itself through the cultural agenda of Islam and Arabism. This ploy has effectively lured those who identify with Islam and Arabism, promising them power and wealth so as consequently to involve them in complicity. This is also why we depict it as Islamo-Arabist, which is of purely ideological relevance (*ibid*).

The cultural relegation of the periphery will eventually end up as developmental relegation and vice-versa. Having poverty and underdevelopment almost everywhere in the Sudan, one can rightly conclude that all the people of the Sudan are marginalized. This is true! It is also true to say that certain cultural and ethnic groups are marginalized culturally as their non-Arab cultures, languages and modes of life are intentionally being targeted by the pro Islamo-Arab ideological state. This means that these cultural and ethnic groups suffer from double marginalization, developmental and cultural. This may imply that only Sudanese people sticking to their African identities are targeted by marginalization. But this also is wrong! (*ibid*)

One of the aims of this book is to show that the Arabized people of Sudan are in fact being victimized right at the moment when they are deluded into thinking themselves as winners. This is because the parameters of centralization are embedded in the marginalization of the whole Arabized Sudan to the big centre, i.e. Arabs proper. Where the process of prestigmatization is cultural, the process of stigmatization, however, is racial. Swung upon this paradoxical axis, the ideology of domination is characterized by high 'maneuverability'. If accused of being anti-African/pro Arab, the case of the Rashāyda and other pastoralist nomads such as the *Baggāra* (literally meaning in Arabic "cow-herders") will be brought forward. On the other hand the accusations of being anti-Arab will be balanced with the accusations of being anti-African, and so on. This game, which is based on deception and alienation, has been going on for the last five centuries. It has its indigenous factors as well as its foreign factors, such as the Turco-Egyptian and British-Egyptian colonial rules. It may be true that all the people of Sudan are marginalized by default. However, at the end of the day, it is the self-awareness of the individual as well as the group that determines where to stand with regard to the centre vs. the margin.

2.3.1. The Melting Pot Perspective

A discourse of unity will opportunely come into shape. As different ethnic groups from the periphery are being culturally reproduced in the middle of urban areas, the mixture is hailed to be a genuine Sudanese construct. Hence we have the perspective of the melting pot as the backbone of the discourse of national unity, i.e. the process of assimilation. However, being based originally on the processes of stigmatization vs. prestigmatization, it will always fall short of achieving national integral unity up to the moment even when the assimilation is done.

The jet-blacks of Sudan who have been completely assimilated in the Islamo-Arab ideology culturally and religiously are not only being racially discriminated against, but are still stuck with the stigma of slavery and consequently are being dehumanized. This is so because the whole process is built on contradiction and paradox: where the process of prestigma would draw the people toward pro-Arab culture and Islam, the process of stigma would keep dismissing them on racial grounds. One can acquire a new culture in a relatively short time, but one can hardly change one's colour. So blackness is always taken as a stigmatic clue to slavery. It is very usual to hear a dark-skinned Sudanese assuring others that there are members of light-skinned colour in the family.

2.4. The Circular vs. the Linear Polarization

It is clear that the model of ideological polarization is a circular one represented in a centre working hard to assimilate the margin, and a margin fighting hard to dismantle the centre. This model engages the realities of pluralism represented in both the middle and periphery; where the middle can be called Sudano-Arab as it consists of the Arabized Sudanese, the periphery can be called Sudano-African as it consists of those who have their African languages and who have their homelands either in the north, south, east or west. The concepts of "periphery vs. middle" and "rural vs. urban" have nothing to do with the process of centro-marginalization as they reflect normal realities. However, the terms "centre" and "margin" reflect the ideological manipulation of the reality.

Although it seems to be reduced into dual form, the circular polarization, however, is rather pluralistic, not dualistic. The social arenas of the middle/centre and periphery/margin have their respective internal differentiations and strata, because they contain the nuclei of pluralism. This makes the circular model of polarization qualified to manage situations of multi-culturalism as in the case of the periphery/middle and the margin/centre alike. In the natural context of periphery vs. middle, the circular polarization is manifested in a dynamic and dialectical process of alliances between the individual entities of the periphery from one side and their countering entities of the middle and vice-versa. The cultural inter-relations and the linguistic and ethnic boundaries will be the tools for this healthy ideological interplay of acculturation. In the unnatural case of centro-marginalization, the circular model is the only mechanism that can effectively bring the different entities of the margin together against the already fortified centre.

The process of centro-marginalization targets the reality of middle/periphery and urban/rural through the mechanisms of stigmatization and prestigmatization. The elitist centre poses to represent the middle in order to make itself attractive and acceptable and, at the same time, to entice the middle and getting it hooked by using the processes of prestigmatization as a bait. On the other hand it lures the people from the periphery to join the membership of its high club through cultural reproduction, so as to rid them of the stigma of the relegated margin as represented in this twisted way by Africanism. The middle and periphery, Sudano-Arabism, and Sudano-Africanism, are living realities and there is nothing wrong with them. The bad side of the game is the process of centro-marginalization, where the middle will be equated with the centre of power and wealth, and the periphery equated with the margin, which becomes more and more relegated every day. There is no way that the people of the middle would be beneficiary of the process of centro-marginalization whose circles will keep infinitely narrowing until a handful of people remain, representing nobody but themselves.

As mentioned above, this mechanism has been working for five centuries. One may wonder how it is that the people of Sudan have been living under the yoke of centro-marginalization for so long. The short answer is: by being subject to the operating vehicles of prestigma and stigma. The centre has never posed as an elitist one of wealth and power facing a margin of laity. It is, rather, a bloc of free and noble people of Arab origin linearly divided from another bloc of slaves and degenerate people of black African origin. By this tactic it does not only neutralize the people of the middle, i.e. the Sudano-Arab, but also turns them into accomplices. When it comes to the people of the periphery, i.e. the Sudano-Africans, it neutralizes them by linearly stratifying their stigmatization further. According to the process of the stigma, the Sudano-African people – the most marginalized – are not equally stigmatized. In this regard, quoting George Orwell in *Animal Farm*, some of them are more equal than others!

2.5. The Degrees of Stigma

The more black you are and the more African you are, the more stigmatized you become. The levels of stigma go from high to low degrees as follows: African features (thick and broad nose and lips, and fuzzy short hair) – blackness – an African language – and lastly being a non-Muslim. The most stigmatized are those who combine the four degrees of stigma, like the sliding majority of Southern Sudanese. The Africans of Nuba Mountains and South Blue Nile come immediately after the Southerners. Then come the peoples of Western Sudan regardless of their different tribal affiliations, and of whom the most stigmatized people are those who are originally from either Central or Western *Bilad al-Sudan*, like the Fulani and Hausa, etc. Then come the

Beja people of Eastern Sudan who, although light-skinned, have their own non-Arabic language and are very poorly educated and can hardly speak either standard or colloquial Arabic fluently. Furthermore, they are Bedouins leading a life that is – according to the unjust evaluation of the centre – very backward at its best.

The last to come are the Nubians in Northern Sudan who are the least stigmatized for one main reason. The people of the middle, generally speaking, are nothing but the descendants of Arabized Nubians, with some survivals of Christian customs still maintained in their cultures. Nothing is wrong with the Nubians of the North except their twisted tongue, i.e. their language, which clearly reveals their African origin. In fact all the people under the stigma have their non-Arabic languages, or *ruṭāna*, i.e. the equally infamous, colonial derogatory term "vernacular".

In Arabic the word *ruṭāna* means the incoherent utterance like that of birds and animals, or the language of the birds, and this shows how Sudanese African people are being dehumanized. Some people of the Maḥas of middle Sudan, one of the last of the Nubians groups to be completely Arabized, now vehemently deny having ever been speakeres of any *ruṭāna* – they claim to be of Aws and Khazraj, two antagonistically neighbouring tribes in ancient Arabia. One may wonder: why both of them? The fact is that only 100 years ago their elders used to speak the *ruṭāna* of the Maḥas, i.e. a Nubian language.

2.5.1. The South: First Degree

The linear polarization works by securing the neutralization of less stigmatized groups – by making them identify with the centre – in its offensive against the most stigmatized, in this instance, African Sudanese of the South. A line will be drawn so that the whole Sudanese people will be grouped on one side against the people of Southern Sudan who will be grouped on the other side. This is the linear demarcation of the North vs. the South, which will eventually give way to the stereotype that all the people of the North are homogenous ethnically, culturally, linguistically and religiously, which is also false.

All the affinities that pull the people of the margin together, especially with those of the South, will be obliterated officially and unofficially whether in mass media or education. The word "slave" will be synonymous with "southerner". Lured by the false prestigma thus bestowed on them, people from other areas of the margin will flamboyantly adopt the racial bigotry of the centre against the

Southerners. Ironically, some of them later will be the spearheads of the movement of Pan Arabism in the Sudan.

2.5.2. The Nuba and South Blue Nile: Second Degree

Next in the stigma come the people of Nuba Mountains and South Blue Nile. The historical, ethnic and linguistic evidence that relate people of Nuba Mountains to their brethren in the far North, i.e. the Nubians, are either obliterated or merely mentioned in passing, if ever. The argument goes as follows: they are different by the virtue of having different names that may confusingly sound similar: Nuba vs. Nubians, in Arabic: *Nūbāwī* vs. *Nūbī*. The information pertaining to the ethno-linguistic relationship that ties them together can only be learnt in post-graduate studies and highly specialized textbooks and only in one or two of the Sudanese universities. To linearly relegate the people of the Nuba Mountains even more, all through the Turco-Egyptian, Egyptian-British and national ruling regimes, their region has never been recognized in official documents as "Nuba Mountains" as they are dubbed "South Kordufan". To recognize the toponym, which is drawn from the ethnonym, might give a boost to the awareness of their Nubian identity. Being blacks, with their own *ruṭānas* and a legacy of slavery, paganism and Christianity and finally being southerners of some northern Kordufan ... that is enough to qualify them for the stigma along with the people of the South.

The case of the Funj, Hamaj, Ingassana, Uduk and other small ethnic groups tells us more than the case of the Nuba. Like the Nuba, the region of the people of the Funj and these other ethnic groups is also dubbed "Southern Blue Nile", though without ever recognizing the real toponym that clearly relates them to the Funj sultanate. The first tactic is to strip from them the prestigma of being the people who founded the first Islamic and Arabic-oriented state in the Sudan. Another derogatory name is to call them *Hamaj*, literally meaning the barbarous. Being like the Nuba Mountains regarding the above-mentioned characteristics, i.e. being true Africans, they end up with the same degree of stigma. As they live in the hinterland of the highly Islamized and Arabized middle area, hedged by their mountains and engulfed by almost 99% illiteracy, they have always maintained a low profile. Part of the tactic of relegation has been to leave them unbothered so as to let them be enveloped by oblivion. That was the case until they took to arms in 1985 and joined the ranks of the SPLM/SPLA.

Both the regions of Nuba and Funj were linearly relegated as *via media* regions to other greater regions of the stigma – the Funj with the South, and the Nuba with the West, which will be dealt with below.

2.5.3. *Al-Gharrāba* (Darfurians): Third Degree

A linear demarcation that discriminates against the African peoples of Western Sudan is conveniently made when there is a need to target them with the process of the stigma. They are labelled "*al-Gharrāba*", i.e. the "Westerners". But the "Westerners" are not linearly balanced by the "Easterners"; they are rather balanced by "*awlād al-baḥar*", i.e. the "riverain people" which equates with another term heavily loaded with the ideology of power; that is "*awlād al-balad*", i.e. the "people or masters of the country", which is also equated with "*awlād al-'Arab*", i.e. the "Arab people". Although living on the banks of the Nile, the Shilluk, Nuer, Dinka and Funj have not merited the description of "*awlād al-baḥar*". The term is reserved for the prestigma, a status they are unqualified for as they are held as stigma. The *Gharrābas* themselves are linearly demarcated: the *Gharrābas* who are indigenous Sudanese like the Fur, Daju, etc.; and the *Gharrābas* who are not indigenous Sudanese, i.e. those who have originally migrated from Central and or Western *Bilād al-Sūdān*, such as the Fulani, Hausa etc. This group is the most stigmatized, simply because originally they were immigrants, as if the Arabs are indigenous Sudanese. Historically, the Hausa, Bergo and Berno began settling in the Sudan before the Arabs.

2.5.4. The Beja and Nubians: not yet prestigma

The people of the East (the Beja) and the North (the Nubians) come last as they, colour-wise, do not look different from the prestigmatized people of the middle. As the battle against the most stigmatized groups mentioned above has not been completely won yet, the escalation of stigma against the Beja and the Nubians is held back, at least for the moment. Their relegation is restricted to only two aspects, namely the language (*ruṭāna* or twisted tongue, or more derisively "*lisān aghlaf*" i.e. "uncircumcised tongue") and underdevelopment. The chain of derogatory names is also endless, such as "*barābra*" i.e. barbarous, for the Nubians, and *Adarōb*, merely a Beja masculine personal name, to which the whole community has been reduced. This reminds us of the same nominal reductionism of "*yā zōl*" (literally "oh you man") employed by the Arab proper to address any Sudanese.

In a situation similar to that of the Funj, the Beja were left to perish unnoticed from poverty and disease in their secluded hills. To add to their misery and stigma, a considerable number of the *Gharrābas* – indigenous and non-indigenous as well – migrated and settled with them. Hedged in by the Sahara at the strip of both sides of the Nile, the underdeveloped Nubians underwent regular migrations to the urban areas of middle Sudan, where they could have been easily identified with the prestigma were it not for their twisted tongue. The ones who have succeeded in ridding themselves of this stigma were assimilated in the prestigma. Their immediate reward was wealth and power. As they are the least stigmatized, they are also the last to be disillusioned.

2.6. The Tactics of Obscurantism and Deception

The centre has so far managed to manipulate the margin by the tactic of obscurantism and deception. The process of centro-marginalization was obscured by the linear polarization lest the marginalized groups identify with each other and achieve unity in their struggle against it. Such identification would have been characterized by circular polarization: the marginalized groups in the north, south, west, east and middle united together in a circle against the centre. (A besieged castle, however strongly fortified, is doomed). Each of the marginalized groups has led a noble struggle against this diabolical machine of relegation within its own realm, but, thanks to the tactic of obscurantism and deception, the possibility of orchestrating their efforts has dawned on them very late, although not too late. In this linear way of dividing people, the centre has managed to keep the only force that could have caused its own demise under control, i.e. the circularly unified margin. One may wonder, to achieve what at the end? The simple answer is to achieve the "big failure" of relegating the whole Sudan into a marginal Arab state. This is the ultimate goal that centro-marginalization can achieve as it will unfold below.

2.7. The Gensis of Centro-marginalization in Sudanese History

Below we will trace the processes of centro-marginalization through history since its inception in the beginning of the 16th century up to the present. One precaution we would like to draw the attention to is the hoax of having the margin/centre concept insidiously overlapped by the rural/urban concept.

2.7.1. The Funj Sultanate

The process of centro-marginalization has been going on for the last 500 years without ever claiming ultimate success. Since the Funj Sultanate (1505AD - 1821AD), all through the successive regimes and up to the present, Sudan has been run in accordance with this process. The Funj people who stuck to their African identity have ended in marginalization and total dereliction; the other Funj people who surrendered themselves to the process of cultural reproduction have ended in the "nothingness" of assimilation. We know nothing about them now. The linear polarization engendered by the mechanism of centro-marginalization has disrupted their society by dividing it into two blocs: 1) the elite class that has succeeded in ridding itself of its stigmatic African culture and language consequently qualifying for wealth and power through complete assimilation into the Islamo-Arab middle of Sudan, and 2) the public class of the Funj who have gone halfway down the road of assimilation to the extent of losing their original Funj language, but could not be accommodated in the high club of wealth and power due to the eliminatory nature of centralization.

The first class got wealth and power, but lost its African identity; the second class lost part of its original identity and became alienated from both its ancient past and the glorious Islamo-Arab present to end up in total marginalization. In all cases neither of them has emerged the same as their ancestor, ʿAmāra Dungus, who was a black African who spoke the non-Arabic Funj language of which we now know nothing- literally not a single word!

Like the Funj, we know nothing of the Nubian language of the people of the Christian Kingdom of Alodia, which preceded the Funj Sultanate (except a few unsatisfactory lines). In fact we know very little of the origin of the Funj. The victory they achieved in establishing their Islamo-Arab kingdom has at the very least undone them. One may wonder, are they losers or winners? According to Jay Spaulding, they appeared out of the blue and disappeared just like a star in the sky. Now the Funj is an enigma in Sudanese studies. The black hole of assimilation and cultural reproduction has siphoned them down into its nothingness. The people who have survived this black hole of annihilation are totally impoverished and marginalized. The Funj model reflects the true outcome that centro-marginalization, linear polarization and assimilation can achieve for the other Sudanese groups.

2.7.2. The Turco-Egyptian Colonial Rule

The infamous Turco-Egyptian colonial rule (1821AD - 1885AD) invaded the Sudan with a shamelessly declared objective of enslaving people and robbing available wealth (gold in particular). Nothing could have fitted more perfectly into the grooves of centro-marginalization with the processes of stigma vs. prestigma. In all contemporary Sudanese educational curricula, this rule has never been described as "colonial". The fact that this infamous regime committed in its slavery raids the worst crimes in our all history against peaceful Sudanese people is taught in a matter-of-fact way without any sense of national hurt.

The lines are drawn very clearly: those who identify with the slaver are not expected to feel hurt; those who identify with the slave will have their stomach churned with agony, and their pride hurt with humiliation. The question is: where does the post-colonial national state stand here? We should not wonder that all this is being done by the state. After all it is the same state as that of the Turco-Egyptian rule and is the same state as that of the Funj sultanate with no change whatsoever as it is running in the same channeled groove of centro-marginalization already dug by the Nubian Chistian states and later by the Funj state and later consolidated by the Turco-Egyptian rule and their ideology of Islamo-Arabism. No wonder it is a state led by the elite class that was created by the colonial systems of yesterday.

2.7.3. The Mahdia Revolution

The Mahdia (1885AD - 1899AD), in essence, was a revolution of the marginalized people of Sudan against the centre, which was occupied by the Turco-Egyptian colonial rule, its accomplices of Arabized Sudanese (pseudo-Arabs) and their growing elite class. Furthermore, it was a revolution where the marginalized forces were brought together, from the west, the south, the east, and the north, along with the people of the middle. In this respect it was a national revolution and Muḥammad Aḥmad al-Mahdi was a forerunner of Sudanese nationalism, decades before it would take its shape. Facing a foreign ruler was enough to catalyse the orchestration of a national struggle. However, being entrapped in an Islamic discourse of fantasy that proved to be very useful in mobilizing the people to revolt, the Mahdia state had no choice but to run in the same groove of centro-marginalization. Where the revolution was national, the state developed an extremely central nature. It tried to physically push the people of the margin in order to reproduce them culturally and even ethnically in the centre. This was facilitated by enforcing migration from the country and rural areas to the capital, Umdorman, under different pretexts. This is how the margin/centre concept has been obliterated by the rural/urban concept. The perspective for national integration or "nationalism" consequently came to be the melting pot.

The Mahdi's successor, *al-Khalīfa* ʿAbdullāhi al-Taʿāyshi, himself of a Fulani origin co-opted by *Baggāra* Arabs, showed a typical pastoralist Arab Bedouin kind of ruthlessness in ruling his subjects. Not only did the Sudano-Africans moan under the yoke of his crude despotism, but also other strata of Sudano-Arabs, especially the historically privileged riverain Arabized stratum. Slavery was once again a state-supported practice. The tragic scenario of Mahdia fanaticism, despotism and slavery would be repeated in Sudan a century later with its impact proportionate to the level and degree of stigma.

2.7.4. The British-Egyptian Colonial Rule

The British-Egyptian colonial rule (1898AD - 1956AD) came with its motto being "divide and rule", which properly fits into the linear polarization model. Where it showed a relative leniency in dealing with the resistance made by the people of the middle, especially the riverain Arabized Sudanese, it was extremely savage and merciless in crushing the resistance of the peoples of the margin, especially in Nuba Mountains, Darfur and Southern Sudan in what is known as the Pacification Wars. We still know very little of the crimes committed there as no one has dared to raise the issue. In the national rule era no one bothered. Aside from scanty and passing remarks, the heroic resistance of the people of Southern Sudan, Nuba Mountains and Darfur has always been absent from our national educational curricula. The British-Egyptian rule manipulated two virtues and almost turned them into vices: academia and Christianity. In its pretense to protect the Southerners from being enslaved by the Northerners, it fell fittingly into the groove of centro-marginalization and its model of linear polarization.

The first linear division they applied was to separate Darfur from the rest of the Sudan. In the Mahdia time the riverain prestigma was relegated in favour of the Arabized people of Western Sudan in general and the *Baggāra* Arabs in particular, whose migration to the middle Sudan was a state policy. Against such an invasion the prestigma created a host of highly discursive and prestigmatic terms such as "*awlād al-baḥar*" (riverain people) who are "*awlād al-'Arab*" (Arab people) who are also "*awlād al-balad*", i.e. masters of the country. On the other hand the people from Western Sudan, regardless of whether they were *Baggāra* or Fur, were derogatorily dubbed in a wholesale manner "*awlād al-Gharib*" (people of the west). However, those people or "*awlād al-Gharib*", succeeded in forcing their way to the high club of the prestigma. Henceforth, it was a model followed on an individual scale by people from Western Sudan to penetrate the prestigma of the centre by various tactics such as co-opting and marriage. This tension between the westerners and the riverain people has not yet subsided. It was this tension that the colonial British intended to manipulate. By then *al-Sulṭān* ʿAlī Dīnār (the last Sultan of Darfur when it was still an independent country from 1899-1916) had succeeded in restoring the kingdom of his Fur ancestors. The British plan was to let him keep his self-assumed monarchy in order to turn him into a puppet. This proved to be a great mistake.

Failing in that, they turned their attention to the South and Nuba Mountains. The infamous British policy of the "Closed Districts" was a linear demarcation that consolidated the stereotype of the South (annexing to it the Nuba Mountains) vs. the North. The British rule pretended to abolish slavery, the same slavery that it tolerated in what it depicted as the North (cf. Sikainga, 1996). That was in the aftermath of the disillusion of the British administration regarding the stance of the Southern Sudanese in their army. In tune with the processes of the stigma and prestigma, the British began a decade before to dismantle what were known as the Sudanese Battalions, which consisted mainly of black Sudanese mostly from the South, Nuba Mountains, and the Blue Nile, mostly with ex-slave backgrounds, and slowly replaced them with what was believed by the prestigma of the centre to be people of "noble" origin.

By the time the British left, the soldiers were still mostly jet-black Sudanese, but not the officers; they were replaced by recruits from "*awlād al-gabāyil*" (people of [noble] tribes) or "*awlād al-balad*" (masters of the country), the same officers who would lead a few years later, just before Independence, another "Pacification War" in Southern Sudan and ravage it. If the black Sudanese officers had been kept, the future of the Sudan could have been different. Completely detribalized from their respective black peoples but still keeping their jet-black colour, they were let down by the British and Egyptians alike to be stigmatized by the centre (cf. Kurita, 1997).

The British and Egyptians could not feign ignorance of what had become of those people who helped them in their victory over the state of the Mahdi's Khalīfa. To make them utterly vulnerable, they were gradually and systematically stripped of the only prestige and power left to them, i.e. their percentage in the army. They bore the cross of the stigma, even though they were completely assimilated in the Islamo-Arab culture of the centre. People are lured into assimilation by the false belief that something held as inferior will be accepted into what is held as superior. The function of this process is not in any way an exercise of social equality. On the contrary it is a means to facilitate the superior and prestigma by providing it with what can be held as inferior and stigmatic.

2.8. Independence: Who is Sudanese?

The national rule that began in 1956 did not only run smoothly in the groove of linear polarization, but institutionalized it by law. The law held any Sudanese to be a suspect foreigner until they proved that they were Sudanese. The Sudanese people would be the first people in the world to hold, inside their own country, official documents to prove that they were Sudanese and not foreigners. States all over the world take the population in its generality to be nationals, and then tend to control the foreigners who are relatively very few. This is common sense: if you have a bushel of peas mixed up in a sack of broad beans, you sort them out by picking out the peas from the broad beans. The successive governments of post-independent Sudan did exactly the opposite – they picked up the Sudanese inside the country and left behind the foreigners. Up until now, 62 years after independence, far fewer than 15 million people have proved that they are Sudanese in this linear demarcation way of establishing nationality. This strange nationality law is nothing but a ploy of obscurantism and a tool of deception and alienation. What is the criterion of nationality adopted by the successive governments in the censuses undertaken since independence? According to the last ones undertaken in the 1990s and 2000s, a figure of at least 40 million is given for the total population of old Sudan. These are two systems that defeat each other, but are simultaneously adopted for a reason. According to this law, all the marginalized Sudanese are officially not considered Sudanese until they prove otherwise.

The linear significance of the law in classifying the people as stigma vs. prestigma becomes clearer as its first victims are always those whose ancestors were immigrants, but not the so-called Arabs (pseudo-Arabs). In the middle of 1976 a Libyan-backed movement of armed Sudanese opposition broke into Khartoum with the intention of toppling the regime. After being routed, it was dubbed by the regime a movement of "foreign mercenaries". Sudan TV made live interviews with people in the streets of Khartoum to show to the world that they were really mercenaries and foreigners from the public's point of view. The standard question was as follows: "How did you know that they were foreigners?" The average answer was that: "They were blacks and did not speak Arabic". The people were not saying this because of their support for the regime. By simply identifying with the centre culturally and socially, they were telling the truth as they perceived it. On the other hand the elite class that was operating the government (its intellectuals of the South included) was well aware of this situation and was making use of it. This will be repeated again in 2008 when the forces of the revolutionary Justice and Equality movement were chased out of Khartoum after succeeding in storming it, coming all along from Chad.

2.8.1. The Sudanese Army

Just as with the history of the Sudan, the history of the Sudanese army is entangled with slavery. The genesis of the present-day Sudanese army can be traced back to the policy of slave-raids of the Turco-Egyptian colonial rule (1821 - 1885). As mentioned earlier, the ruler de facto of Egypt, Muḥammad ʿAli Pasha, decided to invade the Sudan for more than one reason; among them was the intention to mine for gold and discover the sources of the White Nile. But the prime reason was to organize systematic slave-raids deep into the hinterland (Darfur, South Sudan, Nuba Mountains, and upper Blue Nile) in order to capture as many slaves as possible to be used as foot soldiers in his expansionist empire of little Ottoman Egypt. For more than thirty years, long after his death, this infamous policy was adopted, resulting in a huge army of slaves. Under pressure from Europe, the Turco-Egyptian colonial rule was compelled to abandon this vice and later reluctantly abolished slavery, but only officially.

Later, army recruits were made through a kind of watered-down slavery, or more precisely 'slavery by consent'. Tribal chiefs in the very areas that were targeted by slave-raids were negotiated with to voluntarily nominate a certain number of youth for enlistment. They were not literally slaves, but they were also not free to refuse recruitment or otherwise their chiefs were going to answer for that. A particular name for them was conveniently coined, i.e. "*al-jihādiyya*", an Arabic plural adjective derived from "*jihād*", indicating the fighting nature of those soldiers and subsequently their *Jihādiyya* officers.

When the Mahdia revolution took place (in 1885), part of the *jihādiyya* (officers and soldiers alike) joined the ranks of the army of the revolution only to defect a little later in large numbers but not without a great toll that was inflicted upon them by the revolutionary army. The other part of them, who were steadily loyal to the Khedive in Egypt, stood against the revolution and eventually headed back to Cairo. They stayed there to come back to the Sudan in 1898 as part of the invading army of Kitchener who defeated the Mahdia state and established the so called Condominium Rule (1899 - 1956). This time they came under the appellation "Sudanese battalions" (*al-ōrṭāt al-Sūdāniyya*) (cf. Al Awad, 1980). The Sudanese battalions played a crucial role in defeating the Mahdist regime; they were the first forces of the invading army to reach Omdurman, the capital, and subjugate it. They came to this with a well-nursed vendetta.

The soldiers of the Sudanese battalions were maybe the first generation of Sudanese people to be collectively subjected to outer influence, in particular the North African, Ottoman, and European civilizations. No wonder they came back to the Sudan and rightly posed as the spearhead of modernity. Nationalism was among the modern notions they came back with, among others. Understandably, they proved to be more committed to the national issues of the Sudan than the infant elite class, which was forming very largely out of the graduates of the newly established vocational secondary school of Gordon Memorial College (established in 1900). At the beginning the colonial rule was counting very much on this class formed by the descendants of yesterday's slaves in addition to the pacified soldiers from other ethnicities of the North (such as the Shāygiyya) who had proved their loyalty to the them in the war against the Mahdist regime. This reliance was extended to the soldiers and officers who graduated from the military college, most of which were the descendants of the Sudanese battalions.

As said above, the descendants of the Sudanese battalions, whether soldiers or graduate officers of the military college, pioneered the national movement. The White Flag anti-colonialist organization which is considered to be the first nationalist movement in the modern history of the Sudan was mainly indebted to this class. In 1924, the White Flag led a civilian and military revolt against the Condominium colonial rule. It was swiftly crushed but not without stirring national sentiments among a wide range of Sudanese people. That was the moment when the colonial rulers became aware that the descendants of the Sudanese battalions were funneling the anti-colonial sentiments. That was also their moment of disillusion. Thenceforth, they would steadily change their tactic so as to undermine this patriotic class.

In 1925, the Sudan Defense Force was established, in fact out of the Sudanese battalions but not to serve the same ends. The tactic was very simple: the soldiers were mostly from those areas that were previously the direct target of slave-raids, but the officers were not. Instead of recruiting its officers from those areas, the new force drew its recruits from the middle and northern riverain Sudan. While the soldiers belonged to the stigma, the officers belonged to the prestigma. This was the genesis of the present-day Sudanese army.

This new development would prove to be crucial as the interplay between democratic governments led by the prestigma vs. military dictatorial regimes led by the prestigmatic military officers would shape the future of 20th century Sudan. The Sudanese army would prove to be the only army in history that has never fired a single bullet against an outside army. All its battles are against its own people, i.e. the very people it is supposed to protect. In October 2012, the Israeli air force bombed a military plant known as *al-Yarmūk*, about 20 km south of Khartoum, as it suspected it of having connections with Iranian illicit arsenal manufacturing in the Sudan. In response to that, the Sudanese army spokesman retorted that there was no reason whatsoever for that assault as that factory used to manufacture weapons for internal use only [*sic*].

This draws attention to the reasons that made Julius Nyerere dissolve the army upon an aborted coup. He reasoned that that was an army founded by the colonial forces to serve the colonial agenda. The national rule inherited it as a de facto army. If the national era needed to be protected by an army, then that army should be the child of the national era. And that was the birth of the national army of Tanzania. One cannot but wonder how much Sudan was - and still is - in need of the wisdom of the old teacher of Africa, Julius Nyerere.

2.8.2. Education

The aim of education is mainly to provide the concerned society with its leaders (intellectual capacity) and the development of technology (vocational capacity) that will make life prosperous with regard to freedom, justice and peace. Education, in its broad sense, is to build the nation, not to fill specific government job gaps. Any job-oriented education is vocational, be it medicine, engineering, plumbing, carpentry etc.

The assumption that the Sudan is an Arab nation has coloured the educational systems, traditional or modern, all through the last five centuries. During the Funj era, though very traditional from an Islamic and Arab point of view, the objectives of education were still on the right track as they were mainly sought to provide the nation with its leaders. The graduates of the religious schools (*Khalwa*, which is a kind of Islamic primary school) were not prepared to fill any specific job other than setting up their respective teaching circles and playing the role of local leaders in their respective localities. Having the Islamic jurisprudence schools and Arabic language as its main subjects of teaching that educational system was understandably running in the groove of Islamo-Arab ideology and consequently the centro-marginalization. However, functionally, it was doing its principal job of qualifying local leadership. Further, the tenets of Islam that were taught followed the doctrine of popular Islam (Yahia, 1985).

During the Turco-Egyptian rule a new system of education was introduced whose main objective was to qualify the young generation of the middle riverain Sudan to fill the various government petty jobs. A by-product of this educational system was the introduction of orthodox Islam as the teachers of Islamic subjects were all graduates of al-Azhar mosque-university who followed the orthodox doctrine strictly. From that time education would continue engendering a class of elites (the *Effendis*) whose main esteem resulted from the glories of well-paid government jobs and an elementary education tinted with the orthodox Islamic orientation (Nāṣir al-Sīd, 1990).

A few years after the advent of the 20th century, the British-Egyptian condominium rule began introducing a modern educational system (Beshir, 1969), a matter that eventually developed into the establishment of the Institute of *Bakht al-Ruḍa* which shouldered the responsibility of designing educational curricula for elementary and intermediate schools until the 1970s. The Institute of *Bakht al-Ruḍa* is considered a source of educational expertise in the region. However, it suffered from one fundamental deficiency: it took the Sudan to be a mono-cultural Arab nation. The Sudanese folklore, which could have revealed the true multi-cultural identity of the Sudan, never appeared in its educational curricula. The ancient history and literature of Arabia have been taught in flamboyant detail, a fact that was meant to imply the Arab identity of the Sudan. This has kept going on in a country where in the mid-1970s a post-graduate department was established to teach folklore, then the only fully-fledged department of folklore of its kind in Africa and the Middle East.

The Institute of *Bakht al-Ruḍa* did make some acknowledgement of the cultural and ethnic diversity of the Sudan, reflecting the ways and modes of living and life in many parts of the Sudan. Among many, the main shortcoming of this study programme was that a huge region such as the South Sudan was illustrated by only one little town (Yambio). The whole of Darfur, a region the size of France, did not merit the attention of the curricula of *Bakht al-Ruḍa*. Many other regions were also missing. The curricula kept changing according to the political changes. Moreover, the state interventions in curriculum design, especially during the military regimes, were characterized by extreme ideological orientations of Islamo-Arabism, something the succeeding democratic regimes would not bother to reconsider, let alone do anything.

In a country where millions of children grow up without being able to utter a word in Arabic, the successive governments have recognized no language other than Arabic, whether in education, judiciary or culture. 'Arabicization' has been the backbone of education. This is how education has been manipulated to the extent of turning it into a carrier of the Islamo-Arab ideology, which is highly coloured with bigotry, prejudice and racism, i.e. the legacy of slavery. Southern Sudan has suffered greatly from this educational policy of mono-culturalism (cf. Sanderson & Sanderson, 1981). It is little wonder that the standard of education has kept deteriorating and, consequently, everything in Sudan has been proportionately and steadily deteriorating.

The consequences of the educational process are shown in the bad treatment the indigenous African people of Sudan are receiving at the hands of its Arabized people and governments. The educational system, along with other institutions, should be held responsible for the civil war and the genocide that has followed. It has never dawned on the pseudo-Arab ruling elite that prosperity is directly related to education, and that the Sudan, being multi-cultural, needs an educational system based on multi-culturalism. For them education has been a tool for assimilation.

2.8.3. The *Mondukuru* Intellectuals

With the rise of the movement of the graduates of intermediary schools and the Gordon Memorial College (later Khartoum University) an intellectual movement also came into being. Until long after Independence, the intellectuals of that time did not show in their writing and thinking the slightest awareness of any African depth pertaining to their own Sudanese identity. There are very few exceptions that are related in one way or another with individuals belonging to the margin. The multi-ethnic, multi-linguistic and multi-cultural Sudan of today, which is very ancient, is absent in the writings of those intellectuals who would later take over from colonial rule.

The Sudan is reflected in the anthem of the Graduates Congress (composed in standard Arabic by Muḥyi al-Dīn Ṣābir, a Nubian who actually began learning Arabic in school and Khiḍir Ḥamad, also a Nubian) in a verse that reads: "We are a nation whose origin goes back to the Arabs". They did not only take for granted the Arabized middle as representing the whole of Sudan, but further completely identified with the Arabs proper. They would have been honoured with fairness, if they had limited the frontiers of their Sudan to only that. However, they also took for granted to be the rulers of the Arabized middle Sudan and the not yet Arabized, African peripheral Sudan as well without at least verbally acknowledging the partnership of Africanism in the Sudanese identity. If we leave the West, leave the East, and forget about the North whose intellectuals excelled themselves in the art of complicity, what about the South? How did they plan to deal with the South? No wonder at long end in 2011, it has split off to constitute the youngest independent nation in the world: the Republic of South Sudan.

A few years before Independence (in 1947) at a conference in Juba, the leaders of the South collectively decided with profound African wisdom that they did not want separation; they did that knowing that the *mondukuru* (the pseudo-Arab Sudanese or Arabized in Southern Sudanese Dinka language) were going to rule them. While they came to independence clean of any grievances of the past, the *mondukuru* did not reflect for a moment on what they were going to do. The *mondukuru* simply operated the machine of stigma, prestigma, and linear polarization at full throttle. First, the linear demarcation was set between the North (the bloc of the free and noble Arab people) and the South (the bloc of the slaves and degenerate African people).

The people from the margin other than the South were left to make their choice between these two categories only. Subject to centuries of relegation and created by the biased educational systems that have flourished for more than 100 years, the intellectuals of other marginalized areas were left with only one option if they were destined to fare well in that unjust time: ideological complicity with the centre. The game was very simple: regardless of your marginal ethnic background, which in other linear demarcations may fall into the stigma, if you identify with today's polarization, which only stigmatizes the people of the South, and if you are ready to serve loyally the cause of hegemony which may alienate you from your own people, then you will be rewarded culturally by being recognized as part of the prestigma, and materially by wealth and power (the glory of the *Effendis* which is drawn from the benefits of the government post).

This is how all those who have ruled modern Sudan are originally from marginalized groups, with many of them ironically of Fulani background, one of the most stigmatized groups. The majority of the Sudanese people are aware of the true social backgrounds of their leaders, but no one dares declare the truth. It is not a conspiracy of silence, but rather a hypocritical trait that results from total vulnerability. To declare the truth means to sever your ties with the prestigma for good. As complying with the prestigma is the widest gateway to attaining glory and high esteem, revealing the truth might not be the wisest thing to do.

Naturally, the marginalized people expect their intellectuals to address their daily needs of survival. The manipulation of the direct needs of the marginalized people takes place when their intellectuals pretend to be doing this. Such intellectuals usually end up in total complicity, where they are used as tools of obscurantism, deception and oppression: in certain contexts their true backgrounds will be revealed as proof that the alleged pro-Arab bias is not true; in cases of ethnic clashes where African ethnic groups are usually being victimized, those intellectuals mediate by proxy for the centre by shouldering the mission of subduing their own people.

In the course of time this group of intellectuals ends up identifying completely with the elites of the centre. This takes place when their children grow up as part of the privileged elite class. The process of cultural reproduction has done its job. Thus posing as representing the prestigma, they excel themselves and others in crushing the stigmatized margin. In this diabolical game, Islam is being manipulated as the legal ticket for crossing the bridge. Where does this leave the non-Muslim Southerners? Not fit even for ideological complicity, there is only one path of vice left for them to follow when dealing with the *mondukuru*: corruption!

2.8.4. The Emergence of Sudanese Right Wing

The centre in general and its social and intellectual elitism in particular, have given birth to the political parties that are generally active in the whole Sudan to varying degrees, but not in the South. Notwithstanding the notion that classifies them to be Right, Middle or Left, we classify them here as the real Sudanese Right as they all belong ideologically to the centre. It is this Right that has ruled the Sudan since independence up to the present. It is this Right which should be held responsible for the failure in managing the crisis of national integration and progress. Its rule of the country will shift alternately from elected governments to military regimes. In a reality of multi-culturalism they will have only one programme: mono-culturalism of the ideology of Islamo-Arabism. The Sudanese Right consists of Islamic organizations, whether sectarian or fundamentalist, Arab nationalist organizations and the Arabized population of Sudan in general who identify with the ideology of Islamo-Arabism. The last group feels very awkward when identified as African, something they do not like for the mere reason of their speaking the Arabic language as a mother tongue. Most of the Sudanese Marxists fall in the last-mentioned category. Both racial equality, which is vehemently adhered to in Islam, and the appeal of Marxism being above culture and race, are manipulated by the prestigma in the process of assimilation.

In both dictatorial and short democratic periods, the prestigma machine had a plan of counter-mobilization to manipulate the low profile endeavours of the margin to battle for their rights by peaceful means. This plan, by dubbing these endeavours as racist, works through portraying the struggle of the margin as targeting the very existence of Islam and Arabism in the Sudan. In democratic times mono-culturalism becomes appallingly indefensible – the governments that follow it usually become a laughing stock with a high record of failure. The propaganda machine of the prestigma, including the state-owned radio and TV, nurtures a hateful grudge against the growing voice of the margin. When it is time for the elected government to go, the military regime will come to push back the margin into the status of stigma at gunpoint. The military regimes will carry out the program of mono-culturalism to its extreme, thus accomplishing the dirty part of the job. Furthermore, it relieves the prestigma from accountability for the failures of its elected government, the same prestigma that will immediately assume the role of opposition to the military regimes. When the season of democracy comes the same politicians of the prestigma will come back as heroes - not failures - to carry out the failing and oppressive programmes of mono-culturalism from where the military regime left it … and so on. The democratic/military alternation is in fact a process for exorcising the failures on one side (democratic system) and realizing achievement with heavy-handedness on the other (dictatorial regimes).

In a context of centro-marginalization and mono-culturalism, democracy is reduced to a matter of technical procedure that in essence lacks the very representation of the people. Elections have never been conceived by the people as their own power exercised on a higher level of delegation. It has been taken by them as a political game where the prestigmatic politicians assume low profile postures until they are elected, after which they resume their aloof and high profiles.

2.8.5. The *Mondukuru* Governments of the Right

Since Independence, Islamization and Arabicization have been shared in common by the successive governments as state-dictated policies (Al-Sīd, 1990). Taking the Islamized and Arabized middle of Sudan as representing the whole country prompted this. The post-independence governments dealt with the Sudan as consisting of (a) the noble Arabs (aka pseudo-Arabs) of the middle, (b) the Muslim Africans (with possible Arab blood) in the periphery who are supposed to very quickly undergo the process of Arabization to be honoured with this pseudo-Arabism, and (c) the slaves (those who have not yet undone their black Africanism with a touch of Islam and/or a drop of noble Arab blood) who have no place so far on the seats of power. If allowed, the prestigma, immediately after independence, would have created an institutional apartheid state in the Sudan. However, this was realized fifty-five years later at the dawn of the separation of South Sudan in 2011 when Sudan was officially declared an apartheid state by stripping nationality from all Sudanese of Southern origin.

Being the first sub-Saharan country (i.e. black African) to achieve independence, Sudan was wrongly seen by many African liberation movements as being the leader in the struggle against colonialism. Sudan was blessed by virtue of having one flag out of the three graceful and honourable flags cherished by Africa. The first was the flag of unity proposed by Marcus Garvey (three horizontal stripes of black, green and red) and the flag of freedom which is of Ethiopia being the only ancient African country not to have been colonialized (three horizontal stripes of yellow, green and red) and then the flag of independence, that of the Sudan which was raised up its mast of sovereignty at the dawn of its independence (three horizontal stripes of blue, yellow and green). The three colours represented the Sudan squarely: the yellow for the desert, the green for the jungle, and blue for the Nile. This graceful flag was revered by black Africa as the flag of independence; later when they respectively achieved independence, many of their flags were more or less comprised of these colours and those of the other two flags.

To the dismay of all free black Africans, immediately after achieving its independence, Sudan turned its back on black Africa and ran to the Arabs so as to be recognized as an Arab nation. Rejected by some Arab states, its membership might not have been accepted were it not for Egypt, which always viewed Sudan as its strategic backyard. This prompted a veteran of African liberation movements to say: "Instead of being the best Africans, the Sudanese people have chosen with their own free will to be the worst Arabs". Later, under the May regime (led by Nimeiri, a Nubian who posed as an Arab nationalist [*sic*]), Sudan dropped the flag that symbolizes African independence for a typical Arab-design flag. Many Arab states came to an agreement to compose their respective flags in accordance with certain verses of Arab poetry from the Third Abbassid era that reflect Arab arrogance, chauvinism, and racism at its worst. In these verses, which are of low quality from a literary point of view, the white colour is mentioned as representing prestige; the green colour represents flourishing; the red colour represents epic wars and bloody sacrifices; however, the black colour represents bad luck and calamity (the fate of the enemies of the Arabs). This is the meaning behind the colours of the flag the May regime of 1969, led by Numeiri, had chosen to replace the flag that represents African independence, and which is kept to this day no matter how the regimes changed since then. No wonder some African countries (such as Gabon) have adopted that flag of grace contrary to the Sudan who, since 1970, has adopted its flag of shame that deplores blackness as representing everything bad in life. It was a dismay incurred by a Dis-May regime (by courtesy of Mansour Khalid, 1985), but has since then been taken on board by successive regimes, dictatorial and democratic as well. This shows how the ultimate goal of the processes of centro-marginalization is to marginalize Sudan, and Sudanese people with regard to the big Arab centre.

2.8.6. Corruption as a Political Tool for Subjugation

The successive national governments took up the tactic of corrupting Southern politicians by first preferring to deal with the corrupt ones, and later by explicitly encouraging others to follow suit by turning an official blind eye on what has come to be known in Sudanese politics as Southern-style corruption. For example, a convoy of 200 brand-new government vehicles assigned to the South would mysteriously vanish en route.

The Southern intellectuals were so vulnerable to temptation. Within a whole tribe one could find only one or two people who were highly educated, and those usually live in the urban centres as there is no place for them in the village. In any case the government in which they want to represent their people is centrally limited to the capital. For most tribes of the Sudan, it is considered a great honour to have some of its educated members as ministers, members of parliament or big government officials. The more marginalized the tribe, the more important this becomes.

In the case of Southern Sudanese intellectuals it is understandably much more important. At any given time, the residential compound of a Southern intellectual in Khartoum might be housing groups of people from his tribe who may have travelled to the capital for medical treatment, education or any other service. People of the prestigma in Khartoum occasionally express their astonishment over how the Southerners, like bats, cram up in one house – as if it is to their liking that they are living in that way. It is the southern intellectual's responsibility to have them all fed, clothed and looked after. Nevertheless, the questions beckon: With what? Their salaries? It starts with going to their government seniors to complain about difficulties of life like any other government official, and there the *mondukuru* government is waiting for them with the bait to get them hooked. Those who have already been hooked may lose their bashfulness in the course of time and become bold enough to bargain a price. A famous *mondukuru* statesman (allegedly ʿAbdalla Khalīl, a Nubian black African himself), who originally belonged to a marginalized group, while serving as prime minister commented upon such a case by saying: "Would he [the Southern intellectual] merit this price if a bell was rung on him?" The ringing bell is an indication to the bell of slave auction, i.e. if he was sold as a slave, would he have valued the sum of money he is asking for? And this is how we have the so-called "Southern politicians of all governments", bought with money. Is that not soft slavery?

2.9. A Linear Civil War and a Linear Peace

In the three years of self-rule that preceded independence, the Southern politicians made it clear that they wanted the South to be ruled by its own people in whatever way possible, whether federation, confederation or self-rule. Too excited to reflect on what they were saying in their eagerness to take over from the colonial ruler, the Northern *mondukuru* politicians generously made promises to this effect (Alier, 1990). Holding the Southerners generally as having the status of slaves, they did not take the southern politicians seriously enough to honour their promises. Overnight the Southerners discovered that independence for them meant a change from one master to another, from a foreign master to an indigenous one. It is not easy for any slaves to find that fellow slaves were freed and then made master over them.

The conflict was triggered by what was then called the Sudanization of senior government posts for which most Southerners were not only disqualified, but even the few qualified ones were surreptitiously removed from the milieu of their influence, i.e. the South. To further strip the South of any potential power, the *mondukuru* came up with a plot to disperse the Southern soldiers in the army to different parts of the country away from the South. They were taking precautions against any possible threats or plots on the part of the Southerners – plots that were in fact of the prestigma's own making. Coming into independence with bad intentions combined with short-sightedness, the prestigmatic centre was stupidly projecting its own bad intentions upon the Southerners to rationalize its plots for weakening the South.

To enter the phase of independence from a point of such weakness meant that the Southerners were doomed forever. One year before independence they took up arms. Following the rejection of their just demand for self-rule by the *mondukuru*, they fought to get their legitimate right to self-rule, a matter that not only has never been considered wisely by the prestigma but was further pushed out of its logical limits until it has led to the separation of the South from the North. Immediately after the rebellion of 1955, the *mondukuru* civilians living in the South were chased out and a mass killing of the unfortunate who were caught (mostly *jallābas*) took place, something the *mondukuru* intellectuals will never forgive. Whenever the killings of the South, which are in the millions, are mentioned, they counter them by mentioning the unjust killing of those handful of *mondukuru* civilians in order to achieve some balance.

2.9.1. The Emergence of the Separatist Sudanese Left

By fighting first for the right to self-rule and later for the separation of the South from the historical Sudan, the separatist Southerners emerged as representing the real Sudanese Left. From then on, the struggle of the marginalized groups was always triggered by extreme leftist objectives of separation clearly expressed in their slogans and manifestos. Although naturally born of the conflicting ideologies of Africanism vs. Arabism and the processes of centro-marginalization, the formations of the Left and the Right were enhanced by the linear polarization. It would take a few years for the Middle to emerge and a long time for it to be recognized as such.

As a result of many factors beyond the control of the Southerners, the civil war emerged to be based on the same linear polarization of South vs. North. The colonial rule did not only obscure the processes of centro-marginalization, but it further reinforced it by adopting the linear polarization in its policies. For instance, in what it considered to be the North, the educational system was designed in a way that would only enhance the Islamo-Arab ideology of dominance and assimilation (cf. Beshir, 1968). Where it delayed the realization by the peripheral Sudano-African people of their respective identities regarding the imminently looming marginalization, it accelerated the rate of their assimilation into the dominant culture. This prompted their intellectuals, who were supposed to represent them, to take sides with the centre, thus alienating themselves from their own people. Betrayed by both the colonial British who boasted of protecting them, and by the *mondukuru* politicians of Khartoum who dishonoured their promises, and having the rest of the Sudan menacingly posing as an Arab entity, the Southerners were left with no other choice but to mobilize the Africanism of the South linearly to counter the Arabism of the North.

The Sudanese army, the same army that the colonial British began centralizing three decades before, systematically ravaged the South. Alternately, either elected governments or military regimes ran Sudan with one goal regarding the South: to subjugate it. Where the role of the former is to deceptively kiss the South on one cheek to lure it into a peace that does not solve its problems, the role of the latter is to heavy-handedly slap it on the other cheek. It is very rare for any one of us not to have come across an ex-soldier who has stories to tell about the nasty atrocities committed by the army in the South in the period 1956-1970 and 1983-2005. We may never know all of them as the victims are long since dead and the culprits have kept silent. The Sudanese army must answer to this issue. As said above, centrist scholars always mention the relatively few killings of *mondukuru* with which the Southern rebels initiated their civil war, as a balance for the atrocities committed by the army of Khartoum governments. Without condoning their killing, this can be true only by rationalizing that the relatively few number of casualties of the *mondukuru* are equal to the limitless casualties of the Southerners as a result of the noble race of the former compared with the degenerate race of the latter.

2.9.2. Addis Ababa Accord: A Linear Peace for a Linear War

In 1972 the South, eagerly seeking the self-rule they demanded 17 years before, successfully brokered a peace deal. A year later the Addis Ababa Accord was signed, according to which the Southerners put down their arms and came with hearts clear from any doubts or suspicion to only find the old system of stigma waiting for them. It is amazing in the history of racial bigotry, prejudice and intimidation in Sudan how the victim is whole-heartedly ready to forgive, and how the aloof culprit stubbornly turns down that offer. At last the guerrilla fighters joined the same army they were fighting and their leaders enjoyed the high echelons of government posts they had been denied. A few years later President Nimeiri, whose day deeds never honoured his night speeches, would abrogate the peace accord (cf. Khalid, 1985; Alier, 1990).

Administratively, the South was divided into three districts, with a Supreme Council. By establishing the whole peace process of rehabilitation of the South on the linear polarization of the Sudan, with its parameters of centro-marginalization and the vehicles of stigma vs. prestigma, the Southerners came to be completely identified with the North. The South began forming its own prestigma which was represented in the biggest and strongest tribe, i.e. the Dinka. This consequently led to the formation of a Southern sub-centre with its own sub-margin. The Southerners who fought the dominance of the *mondukuru* for 17 years would not tolerate the dominance of their Dinka brethren. A tendency to pull out from this Dinka sub-centre surfaced, to be immediately picked up by the big centre in Khartoum that already had intentions of scrapping the whole peace accord. The three districts were nominally promoted into fully autonomous regions, which practically made the peace accord redundant. These regions did not survive for long; otherwise they would have infinitely undergone further linear segmentations. This is because the linear polarization could only manage dualistic situations but not pluralistic situations. The South is a pluralistic chromosome of Sudan, and Sudan is a pluralistic chromosome of Africa. If applied in a pluralistic context, the linear polarization will push it into dualism in order to deal with it.

2.9.3. Al-Ḍiʿēn Massacre: Back to Darfur Slavery and Genocide

The ideological polarization of centro-marginalization reached its zenith when people who had a lot to share together began to chase each other; when the prestigma would no longer tolerate the stigma and therefore would manipulate its own prestigmatic periphery as pawn to do the dirty job of physically eliminating the stigma (cf. Hāshim, 2005). And that is how the *Baggāra* Arabs came to commit the worst one-single-day mass-scale crime in Sudan's contemporary history, against people with whom they had been living peacefully for a long time.

The word "*Baggāra*" is a plural adjective in Sudanese colloquial Arabic derived from the word "cow". The *Baggāra* tribes in Kordufan and Darfur are nomadic Arabs who have been greatly influenced by the Nilotic tribes, especially the Dinka, from whom they took cows for livestock, as well as the colour of blackness. On the other hand, the *Baggāra* have also influenced the Nilotic ethnic groups (Deng, 1973; 1978). Highly conscious of their Arab identity (aka pseudo-Arabism), the *Baggāra* are naturally susceptible to prestigmatic orientations, but they are not in any way prestigma. A Bedouin Arab is never considered a prestigma even in both pre-Islamic and Islamic Arabia. In particular, the *Baggāra* can never boast of being prestigma as they are claimed to be descendants of either Rabīʿa or Juhayna Arab tribes; these were the Arabs who committed the *riddah* (apostasy) immediately after the death of Prophet Muḥammad and were brought back into Islam under the point of the sword.

However, in Sudan's pseudo-Arabism, anyone can pretend to be the Arab of the Arabs notwithstanding their clear-cut African origins. Influenced by such orientations the *Baggāra* moved in an anti-Dinka direction for the first time during the Turco-Egyptian rule and the Mahdia as they were drawn into the vice of slavery. Although the rift between the *Baggāra* and the Dinka had already happened during the British-Egyptian rule, they were, nevertheless, kept at bay by the infamous policy of pacification, i.e. crushing the people in order to impose stability. By the time the prestigma assumed national rule immediately before independence, the Southerners declared their first civil war.

The manipulation of the *Baggāra* Arabs by the prestigma as cat's paw had also begun. The dirtiest and most gruesome part of the game was assigned to them to undertake; later prestigmatic intellectuals could easily furnish excuses by portraying them as savage and wildly uncontrollable Bedouins. With the intensification of the civil war, the Dinka who lived on the border of Kordufan and Darfur, such as the Ngog of Abyei, found themselves being held accountable by the state for the war that was going on. The elected government of al-Ṣādiq al-Mahdi (1986-1989) used the *Baggāra* Arabs to punish them. This is how the Dinka and the *Baggāra* Arabs found themselves at each other's throats.

By 1987 the prestigmatic elected government engendered the infamous Popular Defence Forces (PDF) as a pretext for officially arming the *Baggāra* Arabs to fight the Southerners, in this case the Dinka of Kordufān who were assumed to be SPLM/SPLA. The defense minister was an army general from the *Baggāra* Arabs.

Until then the hostility between the two sides was kept relatively at bay due to the history-long interrelationship. Thousands of Dinka who fled the war zone came and lived with the *Baggāra*. In the near past, before the rift was too wide to cross, it was usual for a Dinka-Ngog family to have an inter-marriage relationship with another *Baggāra* family and vice-versa. This is how by the mid-1980s in a certain village called al-Ḍiʿēn in Southern Darfur, more than 6,000 Dinka people peacefully took refuge and lived with the *Baggāra*.

Armed in this way, the marauding *Baggāra* squads of PDF and pastoralist guards (*marāḥīl*) began making incursions into the south, raiding the Dinka villages that naturally sought help from the SPLM/SPLA. The latter came to the rescue with a vendetta. In all aspects the *Baggāra* Arabs were not equal to the SPLA. They began experiencing defeat after defeat. This was good news for the prestigma as it meant that the *Baggāra* were getting so deeply involved in the conflict that reconciliation with the Dinka (the Southerners, i.e. the SPLM/SPLA) was becoming increasingly unlikely. The prestigma was driven too far by its own vanity to sensibly feel the responsibility for saving the *Baggāra* the degradation of this manipulation. The fact was that not only were the Dinka being victimized, but also the chivalrous *Baggāra* as well. As they faced mounting defeats, the *Baggāra* began nursing deep hatred towards the Dinka in general. The rift was widening, the inter-relationship weakened. A certain bitter defeat that befell the *Baggāra* in 1987 at the moment when they thought themselves victorious led them to direct their attention to the peaceful Dinka who were living with them at al-Ḍiʿēn, on whom they sought to take revenge, pouring out the venom of their hatred.

In one single day in March 1987 at least 1,000 Dinka were massacred, 4,000 were burned alive, and the survivors – around 1,000 – were enslaved. The massacre began early in the day. At first the bewildered Dinka did not believe what was going on. When the reality dawned on them, they fled into the houses of their hosts, who were ironically their attackers at the same time. They were dragged like animals out of their hiding places to be butchered outside the houses. Those Dinka who took refuge in the church were killed along with the priest. They ran and took refuge inside the police station, which was part of the railway station, but, alas, the police turned to be an accomplice. They were killed there too. Whether in good or bad faith – as it does not matter – they were wrongly advised to take refuge in the empty carriages of a stationary freight train so they could be taken away from al-Ḍiʿēn. With the trustfulness of totally vulnerable and helpless people, they hurriedly obeyed. Once crammed inside, they were locked in from outside. Caged in like animals they saw with their own eyes barrels full of diesel being rolled toward them. They were burnt alive, all of them! Only then, with the barbecue smell of that holocaust, did some of the *Baggāra* come to their senses. The survivors were only fortunate as to be enslaved. Hence slavery prevailed as the only common sense on that doomed day.

A booklet (ʿUshāri A. Maḥmūd & Sulaimān Baldu 1987), hurriedly prepared by two brave scholars who came across al-Ḍiʿēn by accident the day after the massacre, soon appeared, understandably with many flaws if judged academically. The horrible events of the massacre of al-Ḍiʿēn and the slavery that ensued were related in the book in a straightforward manner of naming and shaming. The first reaction of the government was to condemn the booklet and meekly deny the incident, especially the part relating to slavery. The prestigmatic intellectuals, the enlightened elite particularly, accepted the fact that that was slavery, but they classified it as African traditional slavery confined to tribal wars. Then they turned their full attention onto the deficiencies of the booklet in an attempt to discredit the whole case. Where the massacre merited their *noble* attention, what was discussed the least, however, was the mass burning of the Dinka.

The atmosphere became very tense, with the outside world awakening to the shocking realities in the Sudan. While snarling at anyone who dared discuss the massacre, holocaust or the enslaving of the survivors from a point of view that did not agree with its own, the government declared the formation of a fact-gathering committee. In Sudan it is common knowledge that if you want to destroy a case, you form a committee for it. Discussing the events was discouraged as long as the committee was doing its work. Fortunately [*sic*] for them the coup of June 1989 took place.

The elected government was spared the day of reckoning. The junta took over from where the elected government left off; recruitment for the Popular Defense Forces was intensively widened in an attempt to militarize the whole society (including children) in order to get it stuck with the war in the same way as the *Baggāra*, so they could also nurture hatred against the SPLM/SPLA. Islam and Arabism were abused as never before. In the period 1989-1999, God only knows how many massacres like that of al-Ḍiʿēn took place. Genocide is the most natural development of al-Ḍiʿēn-like massacres that had been taking place in the South, Nuba Mountains, South Blue Nile and Funj Mountains and lately Darfur.

In its reaction to the deterioration of the conditions of human rights in the Sudan, and the reinstatement of the institution of slavery, the West showed an equal evilness. As if drawn to its own past of slavery practicing, it joined in the trafficking of slaves, with hard currency - of course. A British woman with a prestigmatic title and apparently colonial experience in slavery began buying slaves [*sic*] from *Baggāra* Arabs with the naïve intention of freeing them. With the prices of slaves rocketing up in hard currency, trafficking increased as slavery – thanks to the British prestigma – proved to be more lucrative than many other businesses. Far from being concerned with the problem and the ways to solve it, or at least help the victims, the West was keen on demonizing the Arabs, defaming Islam and feeding its ever scandal-mongering press. The self-interested West was settling its own accounts with the Arabs and Islam. Both the West and the Arabs have really ravaged the Sudan, the former by its manipulation of democracy, and the latter by its manipulation of Islam.

After committing the massacre of al-Ḍiʿēn, the *Baggāra* Arabs expected that atrocity to be considered as sanguinary rites of initiation for their acceptance into the institution of the prestigma. On the contrary, they were even more stigmatized by the centre and were dubbed as representing a barbarous Arab stock. If you accept a dirty job, then you will smell of dirt and just like a dirty thing you will be thrown away by the same people for whom you did the dirty job. Desperately trying to identify with the prestigma, and as a last resort, the *Baggāra* desperadoes went to their end by forming an extreme-right organization named *Quraysh*, after the tribe of Prophet Muḥammad. Highly anti-African press releases were dispatched bearing the numbering "*Quraysh* One", "*Quraysh* Two", etc. The only way that would have qualified the *Baggāra* to assume a prestigmatic leading role was to drag the prestigma into this kind of horrible massacre and holocaust. The paradox is that the *Baggāra* Arabs, generally speaking, and as said before, are claimed to be the descendants of the tribes of Juhayna and/or Rabīʿa, but not in any way of the prestigmatic tribe of Quraysh. For such a vanity, a chivalrous African Arabized tribe has turned itself into a laughing stock … to whom, but to the same prestigma.

2.9.4. The Genocide in Darfur by the *Janjawīd*

A decade after the Dinka massacre in al-Ḍiʿēn, the scenario of ethnic manipulation expanded to cover the whole of Darfur and most of Kordufan, i.e. the West, to say nothing about the South, Nuba and Blue Nile Mountains, which were systematically ravaged in the last five decades in regard to human and animal life as well as the ecology. The nomadic Arab tribes of Darfur, riding their horses and armed with machine guns, began committing genocide and ethnic cleansing against the sedentary African tribes. What has happened in Darfur stands as a proof of how aggression is deeply embedded in the psyche of nomadic pastoralists in contrast to the peacefulness embedded in the psyche of settled sedentary people (cf. Cheikh Anta Diop, 1991).

The era of terror of the infamous *Janjawīd* was launched. The term is an appellation of terror with various connotations and meanings, the most famous of which is the one we are citing. The term is a composite word that consists of two corrupted words: *jan+jawīd*. The word (*jan*) comes from the machine gun (GM3) corrupted into Arabic *JīEm> Jīm> Jēn> Jan*. The word (*jawīd*) is from the Arabic word for "horse" i.e. *jawād*, signifying the horse and its rider, engaged in the diminutive form *juwēd> jawīd*.

As both the culprit and the victim are Muslims, the racist nature of the linear polarization, whether latitudinal or longitudinal, becomes very clear. At last the racist prestigmatic Arabs of Sudan have reached the point where they can no longer tolerate seeing the indigenous black Africans of Sudan living beside them. The absurdity is that, in the milieu of the so-called Arab world, those pseudo-Arabs of Darfur will racially be relegated to the stigmatized status of black Africans.

News poured out from mass media all over the world telling how villages were razed to the ground, and how children and women were killed seasoned and then peppered with numerous cases of systematic rape. Based on the narratives related by the survivors, many observing organizations, regional and international, came to point the finger of accusation toward the Islamo-Arab government of Khartoum. The government is not only accused of backing the nomadic pseudo-Arab tribes, but also of arming them, and further fighting by land and air along with them.

All through the decade of 1982-1992 skirmishes and limited killings were commonplace in Darfur. The Khartoum government dubbed them "armed robbery". By mid the 1990s, massacres were launched first against the Masālīt tribe of the state of West Darfur. The governor himself was a Masālīt Muslim Brother who was given orders from Khartoum to let his sedentary people host a heavily-armed clan of pastoralist *Baggāra* who had been driven away from their original home in Chad due to their nasty role as weapon traffickers in the civil war there. Believing the reassuring words of their own son (i.e. the governor) that the *Baggāra* would in no way be allowed to violate the history-long conventional laws that regulate the relationship between sedentary and pastoralist people, the Masālīts innocently and generously welcomed the newcomers. Under the official eyes of the state government, which was headed by their own son, thousands of the Masālīt were butchered in the years 1997 to 1999. Many *Baggāra* clans, groups and individuals of the Sudan, taking side with their Chadic brethren, played a crucial role in massacring the Masālīt.

The fact that the latest genocide in Darfur has been committed by allegedly Muslim Arab tribes backed by the Islamo-Arab regime of Khartoum against Muslim African tribes shows that Islamo-Arabism in Sudan is an ideological consciousness that has nothing to do with either the Arabs proper or Islam. Those are Muslim people killing other Muslim people with the intention of cleansing the land they live in from non-Arab people, just as they did towards the African Dinka in al-Ḍiʿēn, which gave us the twisted picture of the Arabs killing the Africans.

Where the assimilation seems to be a cultural process, its parameters are racial. centro-marginalization is based upon the processes of prestigma/stigma. The gruesome atrocities and genocide, which are presently being committed by the state-backed pseudo-Arab tribes, have in fact been committed for the last three decades in the Nuba and Blue Nile Mountains and for even longer in the South, i.e. since 1955.

However, we must recall that it was the elected government in the 1980s that invented the PDF. It is not only the present Islamic government that is to blame, but rather, it is the successive governments of Sudan that have run the country since independence. In fact they are all one government in kind, posing with different guises. It is an evolving socio-cultural system of governing mentality. The genocide already began centuries ago with slavery. After independence, it targeted the Southerners first, then the South Blue Nile people and Nuba Mountains, and now Darfur. With the noria of genocide operating at full throttle, nothing was easier than to predict the next victims. Following the compass of stigma levels and degrees, one could easily predict where the wave of massacres and genocide would hit next. In February, 2005, in the city of Port Sudan, the riot police and army opened fire on a peaceful demonstration of the Beja people, killing 22. The wave of genocide was heading east and north. Should we wait until it takes place and claims the lives of tens of thousands of innocent and civilian people before we decide to confront it?

The Arabized black Africans are no longer capable of coexisting with black Africans. This is a state policy based on demographic engineering aimed at changing the identity of the people of Sudan (cf. Hāshim, 2010; 2011). This diabolical plan was not confined to Darfur but to other parts of the Sudan, including the north and the east. The South was to go away as it proved to stand firm against all plans of Khartoum governments to either succumb or undergo assimilation.

Waves of pastoralists, Arabized Africans of Chad, Niger, Mali, north Nigeria, and north Cameroon have been encouraged by the government to migrate into the Sudan. Hordes of pastoralists in their hundreds and thousands were officially welcomed by the government of the Sudan between 1992 and 2002. Sudanese nationality and passports were given to those people on arrival. The government armed them heavily and encouraged them to drive away the sedentary black Africans from their villages so as to settle in their place. People who came into the Sudan for the first time with foreign passports are now state governors and ministers in Darfur.

At present, Syrian refugees, and other Arab immigrants as well, are granted Sudanese nationality, but not before paying at least between \$5000 - \$10000 (or even more) per individual that get syphoned down the drainage system of institutionalized corruption. According to the report written by Klaas van Dijken to the Dutch *Trouw Newspaper* (12 April 2018; cf. https://www.trouw.nl/samenleving/waarom-rijke-syrische-vluchtelingen-via-soedan-naar-europa-reizen~ab331b31/), the ringleader of this circle of corruption is the President's young brother (ʿAbdalla Ḥasan al-Bashīr). This is taking place while more than 5 million Northern Sudanese of southern origin are officially made stateless as their Sudanese nationality was stripped from them as a punishment for the separation of the South.

Ironically, the government of the Sudan officially expressed its readiness to resolve the problem of Kuwaiti stateless Bedouins by not only naturalizing them, but also granting them vast lands in the east in the delta of the Tokar and Gash seasonal rivers. These news were reinforced recently when the Kuwaiti officials announced that the government of the Sudan had endorsed the deal for the price of 5 billion US Dollars (cf. the Kuwaiti *al-Nahār Newspaper* "The [Kuwaiti] Stateless: a Safe Sector and Sudanese Passports", 10 March 2018). All this while the Sudanese government vehemently denies everything- as usual! It is needless to say that this 5 billion US Dollars, if paid, will never find its way to the government safe.

2.9.5. The Rapid Intervention Forces: officialized *Janjawīd*

After committing horrendous atrocities in Darfur and in reaction to the mounting pressure from the international community and the UN, which threatened to take severe measures if the government of the Sudan had not dissolved the *Janjāwīd* militias and put their leaders to trials, the government of Khartoum finally decided to take action. Instead of doing what was demanded from it, in 2004 the government of Khartoum decided to officialize the tribalistic *Janjawīd* forces by giving them the name "Rapid Intervention Forces" (RIF). At the beginning, they were affiliated to the army; however, their utterly unmethodical ways of engagement distanced them from the army. Then they were affiliated to the security services. Lately, in January 2017 a special law organizing the *Janjawīd* forces and determining their jurisdiction was passed by the parliament. In this law they have been directly affiliated to the President of the State who has become more and more suspicious of both the army and security services. The shame is that the United Nations has dropped the term "*Janjawīd*" from its vocabulary under the pretext that the government of Sudan has dissolved the force.

A notorious man from a Chadian Arabized tribe who was born there and barely got a preschool Qurnic education (*Khalwa*) and who entered the Sudan for the first time in his life in 1994 was named as the leader of the *Janjawīd* RIF. He was given the rank of general. Since then, the *Janjawīd* RIF has been used to perform certain dirty jobs in various parts of the country. Aside from the shoot-to-kill tactics they have become known for, they caused havoc wherever they go, vandalizing private and public properties, sporadically killing innocent people on a whim. This has systematically weakened the army to the extent that many army officers and judges were publicly flogged by the gangster-like soldiers of the *Janjawīd* RIF without the government taking any measure to harness these wild tribalistic fighters who have been turned into soldiers.

All this has been dragging on and on in Darfur without the international community effectively doing anything to stop it. The indictment of President al-Bashīr and other high government officials by the International Criminal Court has practically counted for nothing. The complicity of the troops of the African Union/UN hybrid operation in Darfur (UNAMID), deployed since July 2007 to help the Darfurians, to the government of Sudan, is common knowledge (cf. the damning report of the UNAMID spokeswoman ʿĀyisha al-Baṣri, 9 April 2014). The extant atrocities in Darfur has become a routine of daily occurence; the Sudanese army commits a big share of it along with the *Janjawīd* RIF as villages are attacked on a daily basis and women are being systematically raped by both forces. A certain village called Tabit, south east of al-Fāshir, the biggest city in Darfur, was besieged on 9 November 2014 by a stationed force of the army; the men were separated from the women and young girls. The women and young girls were systematically raped (cf. the statement attributable to the spokeperson for the Secretary-General on Darfur, 17 November 2014). This crime indeed caused an international outcry, but just that. Up today nothing has been effectively done to bring the known culprits to justice - so far!

CHAPTER 3

Sudanese Nationalism

3.1. A Consciousness in the Making

Being multi-ethnic, multi-cultural and multi-religious, Sudan has posed a challenge in terms of nation-building and national integration. Until the 20th century, the question of national integration was answered by assimilation. Although the legacy of the Declaration of Human Rights goes back to the time of the French revolution, the right to preserve one's language and identity worldwide as part of the package of human rights has been recognized very late. Immediately after the French revolution, minority languages were systematically made extinct by the state in its determination to assimilate the whole population into the French language and culture.

The ancient Sudan was multi-lingual, though various languages in different periods were presumably supported by the State and probably held as lingua franca. As shown above, the languages, and consequently their speakers, are mostly related to each other. The ethno-linguistic pluralism has prevailed up to the present. The spirit of this age is embedded in cultural and linguistic rights, the violation of which will raise more problems than solutions. In this regard, a consciousness of Sudanese nationalism has come into shape but has not yet crystallized into a well-defined concept. So far the public and scholars use the term "Sudanese Nationalism" in a loose manner. Arab nationalists do not tolerate the term used in this sense, as they believe that it contradicts the Arabism of Sudan. In Arabic, the word "nationalism" can be translated as either "*al-qawmiyya*", or "*al-waṭaniyya*"; the former is exclusively restricted to the ideology of Pan-Arabism, whereas the latter is confined to a country-bound nationalism, i.e. in a way a synonym for Arabic "*al-quṭriyya*", from '*quṭr*', i.e. 'country'. Officially Sudan is an Arab state, but only culturally are its Arabized people recognized as Arabs. Hereafter in this book the term "nationalism" will be used to denote the growing awareness of national integration of various Sudanese ethnic groups in regard to the state and the exercise of power and sharing of wealth.

3.2. The Emergence of Modern Sudan

The modern Sudan, which is characterized by officially taking Islam and the Arabic language on board along with the country's very old cultural pluralism dates from the Funj sultanate. What characterizes that Sultanate is the fact that it was a secular State even though it strongly propagated Islam and Arabism. In fact that was a natural development from the Christian kingdoms, which were secular with clear separation between the state and religion (Adams, 2004: 111-124). In the Funj sultanate the religious institution, represented by the Sufi sects, was an ally of the state but not incorporated in it. In ancient Sudan, as was the case in African civilizations, there was no division between the state and religion. The monarch was a principal figure in the religious institution. However, that was not the case in Christian Nubia even though in its late years when it began faltering, many kings were bishops and vice-versa. In continuation of this, in the Funj sultanate the two institutions were kept distinctly separate.

The Funj sultanate appeared during the time when the Ottoman empire was expanding. Besides being the language of the State and science, Arabic was more or less the lingua franca in many parts of the Islamic world. Considering the encapsulation of the faltering Christian kingdoms, the pro-Arabic, pro-Islamic sultanate was a breakthrough. It opened up the country to the outside world and maintained the history-long continuum of the traditional federation of the ethnic groups. Islam and Arabism were the new tools of the ideology of the state. ʿAbdu Allah Jammāʿ and ʿAmāra Dungus were the founders of modern Sudan. They are also the forerunners of the melting pot model of Sudanese nationalism, i.e. the process of assimilation. That was the only perceived way of nation-making, so far.

3.3. Anti-Colonial Traditional Nationalism

The Sudanese people nurtured a deep resentment of the Turco-Egyptian colonial rule. Beside the ruthlessness and savagery that characterized it, the Sudanese prestigma mainly resented that rule because it had turned them into a kind of second class within the strata of the prestigma. The people of the margin resented it not only for slavery and savagery, but also because it showed the same values of the prestigma as a result of adopting the centro-marginalization process. Following the African model of anti-colonial revolution where religious mobilization is vitally involved, the Sudanese revolution also came with an appealing Islamic discourse represented in the Mahdia (Hāshim, 1999a).

Being nationalist in nature, the fact that both the Egyptians and the Turks were Muslims did not raise any contradiction regarding the religious discourse of mobilization to the Mahdia revolution; the employment of non-Muslims as governors' aides was used practically as a catalyst for the revolution. Although basically rallied by people from the margin, the revolution succeeded in bringing together both the prestigma and the stigma as they were both mobilized against the foreign colonial rule. However, the Mahdia state would end up siding completely with the prestigma, thus jeopardizing the nationalist potential of itself as a people's revolution and bringing the country to the brink of disintegration. Later, this would cause many people to ally vindictively with the invading colonial army of British-Egyptian rule.

As said earlier, where the revolution was nationalist, the state turned out to be prestigmatically central (cf. Hāshim, 2015). However, the Mahdi was rightfully a forerunner of Sudanese nationalism, which was still entrapped in the perspective of the melting pot. From then on the Mahdia revolution would be an aspiration for Islamo-Arab movements in the Sudan (*ibid*).

Losing the whole Sudan to the Mahdia revolution, the Turco-Egyptian colonial rule managed to keep the Red Sea port of Suakin. It could have easily maintained the whole Eastern region if it had not been for ʿUthmān Digna, one of the greatest generals and heroes of the Mahdia revolution, but not without a tinge of disgrace as he was a professional slaver before joining the revolution. Led by him, the chivalrous Beja people succeeded in keeping their region as part of this country as it has always been. If it had not been for them, that region would have been turned into an Ottoman littoral state. After the disintegration of the Ottoman Empire, such a state with such a strategic position could have changed the look of the Red Sea region. The European colonial forces could have not missed that opportunity. The Beja people would have been the first victims of this state. All through their history they have been concerned with and involved in hinterland geopolitics. Although littoral and having the entire Red Sea coast as part of their region, they have never been known as marine-cultured to the extent that they do not eat any sea-food, not even ordinary fish (ironically in December 2017 president al-Bashīr granted Turkey that very spot of littoral land with its strategic port, Suakin, as part of his long-adopted policy to give up soverignty over land for political protection [*sic*]).

After the fall of the Meroitic kingdom in the mid 5th century AD, and before the emergence of the Christian Nubian kingdoms, many petty kingdoms prevailed in the Nile strip from Meroe down to Asuan. They were ruled by Beja military lords or generals. The Colloquial Sudanese Arabic is greatly influenced by Bedaweyit, the Beja language. As it is natural for the Beja to be nationalist, it is also natural for the prestigma not to give them the credit for that. The role of ʿUthmān Digna was restricted to his position as a Mahdia general only, and not without hints of his failure to capture Suakin, or hints about his being a slaver in his early years before joining the Mahdia. It did not make sense for the Beja who are historically known as strict followers of the Khatmiyya religious sect to fight relentlessly in the ranks of the Mahdia revolution and state while the Khatmiyya leading Sheikh escaped the country to live in exile as a result of his defiant opposition to the Mahdia. The Beja dealt with the Mahdia from a nationalist perspective.

ʿUthmān Digna would be let down by the prestigma in a disgraceful manner. Captured and tried by the British-Egyptian colonial rule, he spent 28 years in prison until he died in 1926. At that time the prestigma were fighting each other in rivalry to show their allegiance to the colonial rule. A few years previously in the First World War they had signed a Carta Blanche of allegiance to the King of Britain to support the British in their war against the Ottoman Empire. In educational curricula, ʿUthmān Digna is taught as a brave Mahdia general and strategist, but never as one of the defenders of Sudanese independence nor as one who greatly contributed to the making of present-day Sudan. To come out as a Beja man leading Beja people in a national context shows the pluralistic orientation of ʿUthmān Digna. The fermenting germ of the perspective of "Unity in Diversity" was at work here. A few years later the fermentation would also brew in the West, in Darfur and in the South, as will unfold later. As a result of this nationalist struggle and defiant resistance to the colonial rule many people perished in prison. In educational curricula one does not find anything mentioned about them. When they are mentioned, it is occasional, in scanty and passing information only. They are forgotten because the prestigma has got its own version of compliant nationalism to sell. With the utmost respect to Nelson Mandela and his historic resilience, it is 'Uthmān Digna who is the prisoner of conscience of the 20th century – he defiantly spent the last 28 years of his life in prison.

3.4. Anti-Colonial Nationalism and Islamo-Arabism

After the fall of the Mahdia State, the resistance against the new colonial rule continued. Following the African model, it was still characterized by religion. In many parts of the country Islamic movements of the Mahdia-style declared themselves, only to be easily contained and crushed by the colonial rule. Revolting in the Nuba Mountains in South Kordufan, *al-Ṣulṭān* 'Ajabna fought fiercely against the colonial rule. He showed typical Sudanese bravery and boldness in facing death when he was caught and executed. He went to the guillotine chanting war songs and inciting people to follow suit. However, the Nilotic tribes in Southern Sudan raised the strongest national resistance of ethno-religious nature against colonial rule. Local prophets of African traditional religions, such as the Dinka prophet Arianhdit and the Nuer prophet Ngundeng, led these movements. What is mentioned of these movements in national educational curricula is literally nil, not even scanty. The colonial rule took unprecedented measures of brutality to contain the situation, or to pacify the Southerners, so to speak (cf. Lazarus Meek Mawut, 1983).

Immediately after the defeat of the Mahdia State, the British, the strong partner of the colonial rule, accepted the de facto monarchy of *al-Ṣulṭān* 'Alī Dinār who had already restored his ancestor's rule in Darfur. In the repercussions of the Mahdia, the clear linear demarcation – as mentioned above – was *awlād al-baḥar* vs. *awlād al-gharib*, i.e. a longitudinal line between the riverain people and the westerners. This was the same West from where the Mahdi drew his main support, but now it had to be alienated from the Arabized centre. Furthermore, France was encroaching eastwards from West Africa. A buffer state that could easily be mobilized at a suitable moment to fight the French on behalf of the British was deemed necessary. Last but not least, an Islamic State was needed by the British colonial rule in preparation for their war against the Islamic Caliphate in Constantinople.

On the other hand, *al-Ṣulṭān* ʿAlī Dinār had different plans in mind. Although lacking the worldwide vision, which his enemy enjoyed, he was very committed to the Muslim peoples. Declaring himself custodian of the holy mosques in Mecca and Medina, he took on the duty of sending aid caravans every pilgrimage season. When the First World War was declared, the British managed to bring the Arabs of the peninsula along with them against the Turks. Up to the present, the Arabs are paying with blood and tears for believing Britain. They promised the Arabs self-rule after defeating Turkey when they had already agreed with their allies on how to divide the area between themselves as well as creaing Israel. Inside Sudan the riverain prestigma was never so eager to show their allegiance to the British master against Turkey, which was then, according to their own beliefs, the Islamic Caliphate. But to the dismay of the British, *al-Ṣulṭān* ʿAlī Dinār turned out to be either too stupid not to, or too clever to, swallow the bait. The British, in their campaign to crush his monarchy, dubbed him as too dumb, and that is what prevailed until the independence of Sudan.

In the national rule, the complicity with the British view is apparent in relegating the history of *al-Ṣulṭān* ʿAlī Dinār into obscurity. Systemic obliteration marred the notion that a man committing himself for Mecca, Medina and Constantinople would never have let down his own countrymen. Since time immemorial, the milieu of Darfur has always been eastward rather than westward. The expansion of the Darfur sultanate took place eastward in Kordufan (the branch Sultanate of al-Musabbaʿāt). All through history, Sudan has been nothing but the Nile flanked by the west region on its left side and the east region on its right side. In fact *al-Ṣulṭān* ʿAlī Dinār was let down by the prestigma long before the British confronted him. Identifying with the Arabs and claiming tribal nobility, to them Darfur was nothing but a land of slaves.

A few years later (in the 1924 revolution) the so-called de-tribalized blacks of the Sudanese battalions which were part of the condominium invading army would also disappoint the British. The in-service army officers and rankers along with the ex-officers played a major role in the people's revolution of 1924 which was led by the White Flag Society (WFS). The WFS itself was presided over by a revolutionary ex-army officer (ʿAlī ʿAbdu al-Laṭīf). Thereafter, the British would turn their attention to the centre to seek an ally in the riverain prestigma.

Immediately after the First World War the colonial rule began adopting centro-marginalization as a strategy and consequently sided with the prestigma. In preparation for taking over from the colonial rule and while complying totally with it, the prestigma posed as anti-colonial. Middle Sudan became the milieu for anti-colonial national movements, which were generally characterized by Islamo-Arab ideologies. As the Sufi sects were the parameters of Sudanese Muslims, they would shape the national political movement. In order to cope with this situation, the religio-political organization of *al-Anṣār*, formed from the Mahdi's followers, took the shape of a Sufi sect. The biggest anti-Mahdist Sufi sect of *al-Khatmiyya* along with *al-Anṣār* posed as the spearheads of anti-colonial nationalism with their Islamo-Arab ideology and the perspective of the melting pot as its model for national integration. This is how the urban centres became the chemo-cultural laboratories for culturally reproducing the people of the margin.

Umdorman, the second newest town to be established in central Sudan (after Kousti town), was sublimated to the status of nationalist model, not only because it was the capital of the Mahdia state, but because it truly represented the model of assimilation, i.e. the melting pot. Later the intellectuals of the centre, in their eagerness to identify with the genre of home-town literature in the cultures of other countries, manufactured their own genres of town folklore and literature for Umdorman by intensively focusing the state-owned propaganda machine on it. By the late 20th century, when it was only 100 years old, Umdorman was talked of as the most historical and ancient town in the Sudan.

Taking the colonial rule as de facto, the point of departure for this national movement was, first, to befriend the colonial rule and then, secondly, to indulge themselves in a soft and tolerant struggle against it. Where the Khatmiyya sided with the Egyptian colonial partner, the Anṣār sided with the British colonial partner. The former developed a convenient ideology represented in the unity of the Nile valley, i.e. Egypt and Sudan. The latter developed the concept of "the Sudan for the Sudanese", thus aiming at independence rather than uniting with Egypt, and having the British as prime friends. However, the development of both trends combined together, as a proper political tactic, was the brainchild of a certain Sudanese nationalist who, since then, has coloured the whole future of the Sudan, namely ʿAlī ʿAbdu al-Laṭīf. The then growing intellectual class generally either fell into the channels of the Khatmiyya or the Anṣār, but not before getting an early injection of secularism which proved to be really essential in achieving independence. It was ʿAlī ʿAbdu al-Laṭīf who also had made that injection.

3.5. Secular Anti-Colonial Nationalism

By the early 1920s, with the growth of the infant intellectual class, a secret political organization was formed by a tiny group of intellectuals in Umdorman. Named "the League of Sudanese Union" (*Jam'iyat al-Ittiḥād al-Sūdānī*), the society was founded by a group of educated people who belonged mainly to the prestigma. Then, a black ex-army officer who was of Nubian-Dinka origin and whose parents were both slaves, joined the society. Recently dismissed from the army for his anti-British and anti-colonial views and behaviour, ʿAlī ʿAbdu al-Laṭīf was held in high esteem by the Sudanese society of Umdorman (cf. Abdin, 1985). Being a black of Nubian-Dinka origin and having the stigma of slavery attached to him, he was left to rely ultimately on his well-developed views and charismatic personality. It turned out that the founding figures of the Society were relying on the prestigma in their nationalist views and leadership assumptions. Shortly after joining the society, the charismatic leadership and nationalist views of ʿAlī ʿAbdu al-Laṭīf began to show and attracted followers within the Society and outside it, something that did not merit the appreciation of the founding clique simply because his nationalist anti-colonial views were neither based on, nor did they acknowledge, the prestigma. Eventually a split took place that ended in the actual demise of the League of Sudanese Union and the emergence of a new society led by ʿAlī ʿAbdu al-Laṭīf himself and based on his views of anti-colonial nationalism. It was named the White Flag Society (WFS). It quickly began spreading among trusted groups of intellectuals in urban towns (Kurita, 1997). In a relatively short time it managed to recruit anti-colonial activists in almost all the urban centres of North Sudan.

Two factors characterized the White Flag Society in this respect: the first was the secular nature of the movement; the second was the role of the people from the margin in creating the society. Both *al-Anṣār* and *al-Khatmiyya* sects were religious in nature, with internal ranks based on religious excellence, a necessity in qualifying any member to assume public posts. As families that claimed the *ashrāf* descent (noble, i.e. descendants of Prophet Muḥammad) led both of them, their religious discourse was deeply rooted in the institution of the prestigma. On the other hand, the White Flag Society came with a lucid view regarding the secular approach it followed. Henceforth, thanks to the White Flag Society, the Sudanese political movement was put on the track of secularism to the disadvantage of the religious political movements that were yet to come, both Islamic fundamentalist and non-fundamentalist. Thanks to ʿAlī ʿAbdu al-Laṭīf and the WFS, and later with the growing influence of the graduates of Gordon Memorial College to the extent of bracing themselves to hatch nucleus political organizations, the two religious sects were not deemed eligible to form political parties in their religious capacity. The only way for them to attract allegiance was to allow their respective intellectual affiliates to create pseudo secular political organizations disguising the religious nature of the sects that were standing behind them. The tension between the pseudo secular parties and the religious sects mustering the real public support has never ceased since then.

The pioneers of the White Flag Society (WFS) were mainly people belonging to groups from the margin. However, the major backing of marginalized people came from blacks of urban areas that represented the stigma, being jet-blacks who accommodated a considerable number of ex-slave descendants, such as ʿAlī ʿAbdu al-Laṭīf himself. As they were also the majority in the Sudanese armed forces under the colonial rule, soldiers and officers alike, the White Flag Society was in a very strong position with regard to mobilizing the masses against the colonial rule. Therefore, the revolution of 1924 is rightly associated with it. Some scholars may argue against this, but the fact that the backbone of the revolution were the military blacks and the ex-slave descendants should be understood in the light of the fact that ʿAlī ʿAbdu al-Laṭīf himself was a military black man with the same social background.

The anti-colonial nationalist orientations of those black Sudanese, who bore a stigma in the Sudanese society of middle Sudan, made both the British and the prestigma reconsider their situation in the military as well as in the society. The prestigma of middle Sudan was frightened by the leading role this stigmatized group assumed. They felt that their prestigmatic status was being undermined.

The crackdown on the White Flag Society and the revolution it led took three forms. The first was to brutally and unjustly eliminate the leaders either physically or psychologically. Some of those who belonged socially to the prestigma were spared at the last moment as they faced the firing squad. The second was to strip the military of its component of jet-black officers and gradually replace them by people who belonged socially and racially to the prestigma which proved to be much more manageable. The third was to render those blacks, according to the criteria of the prestigma, to what was thought to be their right status by intensifying the mechanisms of stigmatization, starting from

Umdorman, Khartoum, and Khartoum North, after which the other urban areas would have to follow suit. The cultural activities, such as music, singing, etc., of which those blacks were known to have been the pioneers were encouraged by the prestigma with the intention that they would be taken over by their own youth. Bābikir Badri, a conspicuous member of the prestigma, who at his youth flogged young women who tried to make joyful cries in his marriage (Badri, 1955), ended up in his later years inviting singers to his own house in Umdorman to sing for the members of his extended family. The most famous cultural activity of home-library and reading-discussion groups was especially targeted. The old ones established by those blacks (such as *al-Fīliyyīn*, i.e. the Fīlite, referring to al-Sayyid al-Fīl who established the group, also called "*awlād* [the children of] *al-Mawrada*" Group, which included black intellectuals such as Muḥammad and his brother ʿAbdu Allah ʿAshri al-Ṣiddīg) were abandoned in favour of newly established ones (such as "*awlād Abu Rōf*" Group, or *al-Shawqiyyīn*, in reference to Muḥammad ʿAlī Shawqi who established it), which were associated with the prestigma (Al-Kid, 1987). The White Flag Society along with the 1924 revolution was systematically obscured. This is how the Sudanese people, aside from the main outlines, came to know very little about it.

The British colonial rule took extreme measures to lower the position and social status of the jet-black Sudanese. For instance, at Kitchener Medical School, which was opened in 1926, it was forbidden to admit any black student originating from the south, Darfur, or the Nuba Mountains. In 1933, the first exceptional case took place, but not without a lot of wrangling on behalf of the family of the student (Muḥammad Ādam Adham, from the Daju ethnic group of Darfur- his father an ex-army officer). However, the government never employed Dr. Adham. He was left with no choice but to open his own private clinic immediately after graduation in 1937, and he ran it until he passed away in 1990.

In 1946, the next exceptional case of admitting a black student took place. That was Khālida Zāhir al-Sādāti (a female whose family originated in the Nuba Mountains and whose father was an ex-army officer). It is worth mentioning that the families of both black students were not only of military background, but that they also belonged to the Sudanese battalions that came back home with the invading army of Kitchener. Understandably, the leading figures of the 1924 revolution and the revolt of the military school students in 1930 were mostly the children of the soldiers of these Sudanese battalions.

Last, but not least, the British-Egyptian colonial rule, with total complicity with the prestigma, gave ʿAlī ʿAbdu al-Laṭīf a special treat: personality assassination (Kurita, 1997). He was imprisoned after his trial for years and years only to be released after medically declaring him insane. They did not eliminate him physically, lest he becomes a national icon and an inspiration with his formidable vogue of charisma for the whole Sudanese people in their fight for liberation. The prestigma, while knowing that he was fully sane, contented itself in rendering him into the obscurity of madness when it failed in stigmatizing him. After years of detaining him while declaring his madness as a pretext, he was handed over to their colonial partner, Egypt. One could have expected ʿAlī ʿAbdu al-Laṭīf to rejoice after such a move. After all, even if he had been released, he would have found it too difficult to dispel the vindictively spread fog of madness that hung over him. And thus he actually welcomed being transferred to Egypt, a matter that was done in secrecy, lest it provoked the Sudanese people. However, that was like running from the lion only to fall into the hands of the crocodile. There, he was immediately taken to the asylum of a psychiatric hospital, under the pretext of insanity, to remain there until he passed away aged only 52 on October 20, 1948. To add insult to injury, in 1970 the state reconsidered his position by deciding to promote his army rank from First-Lieutenant to Major. Years before that, the Egyptian government had decided to resume paying his suspended pension to his widow in an attempt to cover up the bad way they had treated him. After half a century of shameful neglect, the redemption was figured out in terms of money value, with neither atonement nor apology: typical of a slaver's mentality.

Despite the systematic stigmatization and personality assassination, ʿAlī ʿAbdu al-Laṭīf stamped his presence on the national memory and political practice. As he was the intellectual founder of the concept of the Sudanese nation (as it will unfold below), he went on to be known by the honourable and nationally-paternal title of "*Zaʿīm al-Umma*", i.e. "spiritual leader of the nation". Such an honour was impossible to erase; hence the institution of prestigma obscured him by transforming him into an abstract image of patriotism. Some national and historical television drama even dared to show his exploits, but without portraying him as a jet-black Sudanese of the Nubian-Dinka type.

3.5.1. Pluralism and Nationalism

After being dismissed from the army, ʿAlī ʿAbdu al-Laṭīf addressed the colonial administration demanding freedom and self-rule for the "Sudanese Nation", in Arabic "*al-Umma al-Sūdāniyya*" as comprising all the people of Sudan regardless of their different tribal and racial affiliations. That was the first time in history that the term "Sudanese Nation" was employed with such political magnitude. To counter his letter, the prestigma addressed the colonial administration, mocking ʿAlī ʿAbdu al-Laṭīf and his views and disqualifying him from posing as the representative and speaking on behalf of the Sudanese people. The prestigma did not only allude to his background of slavery, but even clearly stated that only people of noble and honourable origin could speak for such a sublime mission, giving the reasoning that a nation whose slaves are its leaders was doomed. However, the letter of ʿAlī ʿAbdu al-Laṭīf launched the concept of "Sudanese Nationalism", which started to develop from the level of the melting pot perspective up to the level of the perspective of unity in diversity.

Nevertheless, the term "Sudanese Nationalism" was assumed by politicians and scholars to signify the melting pot perspective that represented the cultural project of assimilation and cultural reproduction of the marginalized people in the centre (refer to the concept of nationalism and nation-building in Bekhiet, 1961; Beshir, 1974). The concept, hijacked in this way, had proved to be very abortive to the views of ʿAlī ʿAbdu al-Laṭīf. Later in the late 1970s and early 1980s the term "Sudanese Nation" was used in reference to the perspective of unity in diversity, where no culture was supposed to be marginalized (Sātti, 1981). What distinguished ʿAlī ʿAbdu al-Laṭīf is not only that he was the first to use the term in a political context, but the fact that he used the term referring to what came to be known half a century later as the perspective of "Unity in Diversity". All we know of ʿAlī ʿAbdu al-Laṭīf is what he said or did in approximately four years of his early youth. Even then, he was at least half a century ahead of his generation. A period of 10 years in that early 20th century may equal more than a whole century in past time.

3.5.2. The Path to Independence: the Tactic

The White Flag Society adopted the slogan of the unity of the Nile valley, i.e. Egypt and Sudan, complementing its predecessor, the League of Sudanese Union. Nonetheless, no Egyptian was allowed to be a member of the White Flag Society. In this way, the WFS accommodated the slogan as a matter of convenience and tactics. Rather than only neutralizing the weak colonial partner, i.e. Egypt, it turned it into an ally of the movement of liberation (Kurita, 1997). This tactic would prove not only to be very practical in the battle for independence and freedom, but also attractive to the two hegemonic sects, namely the Khatmiyya and the Anṣār. The unity of the Nile valley was propagated along with the concept of the Sudanese Nation "*al-Umma al-Sūdāniyya*" respectively by the two sects. The former adopted the project of the unity of the Nile Valley for its secular parallel organization; hence its adherents are called the Unionists. The latter adopted the core concept of "Sudanese Nationalism" as a title for its parallel secular organization, i.e. *Ḥizb al-Umma* (the Nation Party), thus making the independence of the Sudanese nation their goal (for more details, cf. Abu Hasabu, 1985).

Later, in the parliamentary elections (which eventually declared independence on January the first 1956), the Khatmiyya-backed Unionist party got the majority against the Anṣār-backed 'independentist' Umma Party. Egypt was very pleased with that result and interpreted it as imminently leading to the unification of the two countries. It was very clear that if that unity were declared, Sudan would have been the weak partner just as Egypt was the weak partner in the colonial Condominium rule. But the Unionists declined the unity of the Nile valley and, instead, declared Sudan to be an independent republic.

Once again, the far-sighted nationalist views of ʿAlī ʿAbdu al-Laṭīf (independence as a national goal and the unity of the Nile valley as a political tactic) proved crucially decisive for the destiny of Sudan. Although younger, the leading figures of the great generation that managed the battle of independence were hamlet peers of ʿAlī ʿAbdu al-Laṭīf. Bearing in mind his charisma, there was no way for them to miss his nationalist and political views. They all followed him without giving him the credit for that. But then, a prophet commands no prestige among his own people.

3.5.3. Towards the Balance of Identity

The national awareness of the centre emerged in the 20th century to be pro-Islamo-Arab to its core. There was no reflection of the existence of non-Arabs in the cultural discourse of the centre. In the literature they produced, the infant class of intellectuals of the centre mostly identified with ancient Arabia, thus alienating themselves from the realities they were living in (Ḥai, 1976). Those who were related to pastoralist nomads (such as al-ʿAbbāsi and al-Banna) marveled at themselves in the

Bedouin-style itineraries they had occasionally made. This led Ḥamza al-Malik Ṭombol, an intellectual who belonged to the marginalized Nubian ethnic groups and had practically begun learning and speaking Arabic when he went to school, to make a call to Sudanize literature by grounding it on Sudanese soil (cf. Ṭombol, 1972).

Independence brought the intellectuals of the centre to face the realities of Sudanese multi-culturalism; election campaigns put them face to face with non-Arab ethnic groups who could barely understand Arabic. To tell those people that they were Arabs surely provoked laughter and did not incite any political support. The parliament brought in non-Arabized intellectuals, especially those of jet-black colour who were very aware that they could only be accommodated in a multi-cultural, not a mono-cultural, Sudan. Data pertaining to ethno-linguistic pluralism resulting from social sciences and particularly anthropology, a science greatly indebted for its existence to studies made on the Sudan, were too much and too compelling to ignore. Independence also subjected the awareness of the Arabism of the centre to test against the Arabism of the Arabs proper, i.e. the margin of Arabism against the milieu and centre of Arab ideology to which the Sudan and other African countries (such as Somalia, Mauritania etc) served as a margin. All these factors contributed to the emergence of the political and cultural discourse of Afro-Arabism.

3.5.3.1. Afro-Arabism: the Intellectual Discourse

The Sudanese battalions, which were inherited from the Turco-Egyptian era, came back home as part of the British-Egyptian colonial army. They consisted mainly of black Sudanese, the majority of whom were either freed slaves or descendants of slaves. As said earlier, after the abolition of slavery, the Turco-Egyptian colonial rule adopted the policy of tempting the black tribal leaders to freely submit a certain number of their subjects for military training along with the above-mentioned group. Their battalions were then known as *jihādiyya* (from *jihād*, in this context meaning 'zealous fighting', i.e. devoted or professional soldiers). Although the *jihādiyya* joined the Mahdia revolution in its early days, they were among the first to pull out. The term was also used during the Mahdia state in referring to its dervish soldiers who developed from *jihādiyya* proper, but not without an Islamic tint. Living in Egypt and other Ottoman countries during the Mahdia, they were exposed to, and consequently influenced by, the civilization and modern ways of the time. Back in Sudan they were rightly the spearhead of modernization.

Customs associated with modernism such as eating at a table with chairs, bread and today's traditional dishes of middle Sudan which were considered fancy food at the time, music, phonograph and later radio, home libraries, and more importantly women's freedom in regard to education and work, were introduced by those jet-black people. At that time, the society of middle Sudan – taking Umdorman as a case – was extremely conservative. Women were confined to the house. Vocal music, as said earlier, was considered – since the Funj era – to be a kind of vagrancy. Although still considered as stigma, the blacks of the Sudanese battalions made their presence felt as the most enlightened and modernized class in the society. People were taking after their ways of life without giving them credit for that.

This situation created an embarrassment for the prestigma as the masters [*sic*] was put in the position of imitating their slaves. In this socio-cultural setting, it was natural for people like ʿAlī ʿAbdu al-Laṭīf to lead that society, especially those who were further armed with leadership vision and charisma- like him. It was expected that the prestigma of that society would obliterate the leading position of such people in the following years.

The movement for achieving a balance between Africanism and that pseudo-Arabism in the Sudanese identity began with this class and particularly with ʿAlī ʿAbdu al-Laṭīf. Over the course of time it was weakened by the intensive stigmatization launched by the prestigma. Some Arabized intellectuals took Africanism for a fashion in their early youth (such as Muḥammad al-Mahdi al-Majdhūb). With independence in 1956, the voice of African Sudan became loud enough in academic corridors to be merited with pioneering studies led by national scholars who began probing the African identity of Sudan in general and middle Sudan in particular. In the early 1960s it became clear to the intellectual class that Arabism alone would not provide an answer to the quest for Sudanese identity. Where some of them went far back to the Meroitic civilization in search of their identity (the Apedemak group), another pragmatic group just crossed the desert into the jungle. As a result, a literary discourse called the "Jungle and Desert group", advocating Afro-Arabism, came into existence.

However, the newly launched Afro-Arabism turned out to be an Islamo-Arab project designed meticulously to assimilate the growing voice of Africanism (Ibrāhīm, 1989). The "Jungle and Desert" discourse declared the Funj Sultanate as the model for national integration, i.e. the process of cultural reproduction and centro-marginalization, prestigma, etc. They came riding their camels in their venture to penetrate the jungle.

That is not to say in any way that the true identity of the Sudan is not a blend of Afro-Arab. But an Afro-Arab identity where the mechanism of Arabization is in control of all aspects of life reduces Africanism to nothing more than lip service. The institution of the state very soon picked up this fake Afro-Arabism for political manipulation. By the decade of the period of 1965-1975, the scientific publications (cf. Hurreiz, 1966; 1977; Hasan, 1973) pertaining to the Afro-Arabism of Sudan appeared only to be undermined by the political manipulation of the concept.

3.5.3.2. Afro-Arabism: the Political Discourse

The signing of the Addis Ababa Accord in 1972, which put an end to the civil war erroneously dubbed as the 'North-South Conflict', marked a turning point in the identity of Sudan as Afro-Arabism was officially recognized by the state. It was hailed in the government discourse and official statements as the true and indisputable identity of the Sudan. Recognizing them as black Africans was the only way to accommodate the returning Southerners. If Sudan was also their country, then Sudan had to do with Africanism.

For the first time in the history of Sudan, the prestigma happened to be largely headed in many key government posts by Southerners, i.e. jet-black Africans, i.e. the stigma. This caused an upheaval in many aspects of Sudanese social and cultural awareness. The prestigma nurtured a strong dislike for the peace that seemed to break up the foundation of their establishment. On the other hand, the African dimension in Sudanese identity was given greater importance, eventually giving way to the breakthrough of a pluralistic approach and perspective of unity in diversity against the assimilatory perspective of the melting pot adopted then by the regime.

The Addis Ababa Accord took place in a context of political contradictions. Backed by communists and Pan Arab leftists at its outset, the military coup of the May regime immediately committed Sudan to the cause of Arab Nationalism, patronized then by Nasser's Egypt. In 1970, both Nimeiri of Sudan and Gaddafi of Libya posed as heirs of the Pan Arabist Nasser, then president of Egypt. In the course of its lifetime, the May regime kept jumping from one ideology to another like a baboon without ever admitting that. Accused of communism at its outset, it ended eight years later with Islamic fanaticism. In 1977, the

May regime managed to strike a peace treaty then named 'the national reconciliation' with the National Front that a year before launched its aborted Libya-backed invasion. The national Front was then led by al-Ṣādiq al-Mahdi (the leader of the Anṣār and Umma party; al-Ṣādiq's name should always be prefixed by the title '*sayyid*', i.e. 'master' in reference to his his family's claim of being descendant of prophet Muḥammad), Ḥusain al-Hindi (the leader of the National Unionist party, an offshoot of the Khatmiyya-backed Democratic Unionist party; al-Hindi's name should always be mentioned prefixed by the title '*al-sharīf*', i.e. 'noble' in reference to his family's claim of being descendant of Prophet Muḥammad), and Ḥasan al-Turābi (the Muslim Brothers' leader whose great, great grandfather claimed to be a prophet in his own right [*sic*]). At the last moment, al-Hindi pulled off the treaty. This made it possible for the Umma party and Muslim Brotherhood to join the May regime. However, the May regime not only kept its constant adherence to Arabism, but also further consolidated it. This simply added to the history-long legacy of contradictions that had characterized the state in the Sudan since the Funj sultanate. The National Reconciliation Treaty of 1977 actually stood as a contradiction with regard to the Addis Ababa Accord of 1972. In such a context of clashing winds, Afro-Arabism was endorsed out of convenience rather than self-discovery. This is how the perspective of the melting pot was maintained as a constant model for national integration while paradoxically maintaining the discourse of unity in diversity officially. The parties that consisted the National Front were the same ones that were propagating the Islamic constitution against which the May coup took place in 1969.

Regionally, Afro-Arabism also proved to be very convenient to the Sudan. The pseudo-Arabism of Sudan and other similar states such as Somalia, Djibouti, and Mauritania (and all the Soudan Belt, or Borderland Countries to use a Pan African term), which served as the margin of the Arab proper milieu, i.e. the big centre (cf. Mazrui, 1971), could only be acceptably rationalized as Arabized African through the discourse of Afro-Arabism. Those were the black Africans who were either dismissed indignantly as a slave-related stigma in the circles of the so-called Arab proper, or tolerated as a sensitive matter and embarrassment (for more about 'embarrassment', cf. Ahmed, 1988).

There was only one way left for the centre of Sudan to fight out its battle of consolidating Arabism internally and externally. Internally it had to make a compromise lest the growing consciousness of Africanism claimed supremacy. In this regard, the tactic was to neutralize

Africanism by compromising it with Arabism. Externally, the centre was very keen to have its doubted Arabism recognized by the Arabs proper. In this regard, Sudan was portrayed as a corridor through which the Arabs could penetrate black Africa as they did in the past through their relentless slave raids. It was a sell-out deal in essence, and that was their way of proving that they belonged to Arabia much more than they belonged to black Africa. Hence we have Afro-Arabism, which proved to be nothing short of a tactical retreat from the openness of the desert, to the cover-up of the jungle. However, it was almost impossible for the state to drop Afro-Arabism in its official discourse, even when it was riding its high and extremely wild Islamist and Arabist waves.

Although boasting and bragging of having both been based upon Afro-Arabism, two contradictory intellectual discourses reared their heads by the end of the 1970s. The first was the discourse of pluralistic Sudan (i.e. the true Afro-Arab blend), and the second was that of the purely Islamo-Arab Sudan. The first, launched by the Addis Ababa Accord in which the intensive presence of the Southerners served as a catalyst, achieved its crystallization in the perspective of unity in diversity. The second was based upon the perspective of the melting pot and gained momentum as a backlash against the Peace Accord, catalysed by the resentment of the prestigma. It achieved its final goal in the Islamo-Arab fanaticization of the state to which the 1977 National Reconciliation was but a prelude. By the early 1980s, instead of progressively leaping forward, Sudan went back 100 years to be ruled by an extremely fanatical and centralized state similar to that the Mahdi's Khalīfa - a false Imam. This regime led to the extreme use of the whip and sword of Islam, extreme impoverishment of marginalized areas, intensive migration from the geographical rural areas to the relatively privileged urban centres, drought and starvation, severed neighbour bilateral relations, civil wars and national disintegration and slavery. Once again Sudan needed a new national leader of the Nuba-Dinka type of ʿAlī ʿAbdu al-Laṭīf to sort out the mess on both theoretical and practical levels.

3.6. The Perspective of Unity in Diversity

By the time of the signing of Addis Ababa Accord, Sudan was officially baptised as Afro-Arab. The intellectual pioneers of Afro-Arabism were given key posts in cultural institutions along with the returning Southerners. So far the State and the intellectual pioneers of Afro-Arabism were still stuck with the melting pot perspective. Nonetheless, the strong presence of the Southerners in every aspect of Sudanese life, political and socio-cultural as well, opened new venues for further probing the identity of Sudan. Debates flared up among intellectuals (1975-1980) where the Islamo-Arab parameters of the state-adopted Afro-Arabism were eventually discerned, thus paving the way for the emergence of the discourse pertaining to the perspective of unity in diversity as the proper perspective to potentially ground true Afro-Arabism. A new movement with a new vision of Sudanese nationalism was 'prospectively' in the making.

As the symptoms of a fanatic fervour began showing on the face of Nimeiri, the head of state, the prestigma institution worked hard to hamper the rising awareness of a pluralistic Sudan by manipulating both the glamour of Islam and the clamour of Arabism in tune with the delirious visions of the new Imam. By the time, (1977) the National Front (Umma Party and Muslim Brotherhood) who were historically belonging to the prestigma, joined the regime, the Muslim Brotherhood was the most ordered and influential among the newcomers as they were highly organized and capable of mobilizing and mustering students of higher education institutions. The student unions, officially declared to be redundant for years, were reinstated by the government to only be controlled by the state-supported Muslim Brothers. The faltering May regime could have dreamt of nothing better than that new lifeline.

Against this background, a new student movement appeared in the late 1970s. Known as the Congress of Independent Students, it declared itself as "a healthy alternative" to all other political organizations: the sectarians (Anṣār and Khatmiyya), Muslim Brothers, Pan Arab Nationalists (Nasserite and Baʿathist) and the Communists. Recognizing itself as the true middle, its political programme centred on toppling the May regime and the restoration of democracy. On the other hand, the core of its treatise of thought centred on Sudanese nationalism as revived and constructed from the variety of genres of Sudanese heritage and folklore. Constantly being subject to bitter criticism and disparage by other political organizations for what was considered as its vague perspective, the new movement soon caught up with the then heated debates of intellectuals regarding Afro-Arabism and its wavering between the perspective of the melting pot and that of unity in diversity. By 1983, a discourse of high theoretization and philosophization was eventually developed within the ranks and files of this movement. That discourse was earnestly developed with its core being democracy and Sudanese nationalism as based upon the perspective of unity in diversity (cf. Hāshim, 1999a and the subsequent editions of 2012, 2013, 2015, and 2018). Soon after its establishment, that discourse began taking huge, wide and long leaps forward; it kept branching out conceptually, critically and analytically until it reached a state of maturity by which it was vividly capable of leveling a damning condemnation of centro-marginalization, cultural reproduction, and Islamo-Arabism - a term coined by it with a purely ideological relevance in contrast to honourable Islamic and Arab cultures. Since then, the Congress of Independent Students has preached its doctrine of Sudanese nationalism as opposed to the doctrine of Arab nationalism officially preached by the successive Sudanese establishment and governments.

The Congress of Independent Students played a decisive and crucial role in toppling the May regime. Immediately after its inception in 1979, it succeeded in Khartoum University (the biggest and most influential university in contemporary Sudanese history) in mustering the various political organizations and led a coalition against the state-supported Muslim Brothers in the elections of the Student Union (KUSU), the strongest political arm in post-independent Sudan. By 1984, it led a similar coalition that ousted the Muslim Brothers again. The following year, the May regime was toppled by people's revolution led by a broad coalition of political parties and trade unions spearheaded and mobilized in the first place by KUSU along with other university student unions headed by the Congress of Independent Students.

Since 1989, while the Congress of Independent Students has diminished as a political organization due to the severe measures taken by the Islamic regime in cracking down on any opposition movement in the Sudan, paradoxically its intellectual discourse of Sudanese nationalism has steadily gained momentum. By the turn of the century, the movement was fast spreading in all Sudanese universities with its discourse of Sudanese nationalism as represented in the perspectives of unity in diversity and that of the margin vs. the centre (cf. Ismā'īl, 2015). Criticism of centro-marginalization and the call for the unity of marginalized groups did not only gain momentum throughout the Sudanese student movement, but also became the core ideology of the "New Sudan", a highly fashionable term engendered by John Garang, the historic founder and leader of the Sudan Liberation Movement/ the Sudan Liberation Army (SPLM/SPLA). As a true Pan Africanist, he drew the idea of liberation from the global call of Pan Africanism for mind liberation (cf. Chinweizu & Madubuike, 1983; Chinweizu, 1987; and Ngūgī wa Thiong'o, 1986).

3.7. The Madness of the State and Holy Martyrdom

By 1982, the state in Sudan was plunging into an abyss of extreme religious fanaticism. Nimeiri, a secular sanguinary despot, feigned sainthood and put on the regalia of Islam as a camouflage. The Inquisition State of the Mahdia type was reinstated once again. Islam was abused by reducing it into a harsh penal code that was arbitrarily applied. The machine of the prestigma was given free reign thus targeting the people of the margin; the blacker you are the more targeted you become. In an unprecedented measure, Khartoum was declared a stigma-free capital. It was decided that people from the margin, who were mostly black African not yet Arabized, be evacuated from the tri-capital (Khartoum, Umdorman and Khartoum North) under the pretext of eradicating vagrancy and loitering. In broad daylight and to the cynical and mocking laughter of the prestigma, the blacks of Sudan, i.e. the true Sudanese, were hunted and herded like animals to be loaded into trucks that took them back to their home regions which were too impoverished by the process of centro-marginalization to sustain them. Simple Sudanese people did not understand what was going on. It seemed to them that the leaders at the top had lost their common sense.

As the targeting was proportionate with the degree of stigma, the Southerners, by the virtue of their true Sudanese complexions, were ill-positioned to moan under the yoke of that apartheid State. Their intellectuals and political leaders, who were mostly Christians, were made under the point of gun to undergo the humiliation of declaring their Islamic allegiance *-sic-* (*al-bay'a*) to the fake Imam. Being already abrogated a few years before, the Addis Ababa Accord was long since forgotten by the delirious Imam.

That was the moment the Sudanese people needed a Christ-like saviour who took their sins and fears and died on the cross for them. A humble, old Sudanese man of formidable intellect and holiness stood up and faced the delirious Imam and then courageously took the brunt of that madness. That was the martyr Maḥmūd Muḥammad Ṭāha, who was executed in January 1985 by Nimeiri, the fake Imam. The insightful Islamic thought and saintly courage of Maḥmūd Muḥammad Ṭāha provided a source of both enlightenment and patriotism. At the moment of execution, his face was uncovered for his judges so that they could be sure that it was him. They were expecting to see fear and remorse on his face, but to the fright of his pharisaic judges, there was a divine smile, a smile of absolute peace and understanding.

That was the example of courageous leadership the Sudanese people were waiting to follow. That was the sublime bravery that revealed to the Sudanese people the vanity of fear. Less than four months later (on April 6, 1985) they took to the streets and that was the end of a mad era. But its end did not come before it triggered off another civil war. "The Sudanese people are a gigantic nation led by dwarves" was a maxim said by Maḥmūd Muḥammad Ṭāha; every day the Sudanese people got more certain of its truism. In the years that followed his saintly death, his thought was to be adopted in piecemeals by many Muslim intellectuals worldwide and the Sudanese intellectuals in particular, without ever acknowledging this (cf. el-Bashīr, 2013). The absurdity of it all is that mostly those who spent their lives fighting his thought practised this piracy; ironically, some of the judges who condemned him to death were among those intellectual scavengers.

3.8. Nation Statehood and Colonialism in Africa

The problems pertaining to the national statehood in the Sudan, itself being part of sub-Saharan Africa, i.e. black Africa, necessitates that to probe it within the context of pre-colonial Africa and post-colonial Africa as well. Post-colonial Africa, generally speaking, has had enough time to build up capacities pertaining to technical knowledge and know-how necessary for nation building. But still they have all failed to achieve this. One of the cynical replies the West provides for this is that black Africans do not know how to consolidate power; they always get stuck with inter-conflicts that keep breaking up the delegated power of governance. The West that holds to this viewpoint does this in order to degenerate the Africans in their generality. This shows how the racism that propelled slavery and colonialism is still strongly alive.

Although it is true that post-colonial Africa is consuming itself in such inter-conflicts to the extent of preventing the bottom-up delegated power of the whole nation to consolidate, the reasons behind this are not innate qualities. To probe these reasons we have to revisit the damage incurred by colonialism, which is in fact much graver than most critics have thought. It is damage that goes deeper, beyond technical capacity build-up and know-how, something that can relatively easily be obtained. It concerns the factors related to the governance institutions, a matter seldom noticed. When Europe scrambled to colonize weaker nations in general and Africa in particular, the primal governance institution, namely the state, was long since it had reached its full maturity of the present-day with regard to the basic concept of 'citizenship'. This maturation of the state took place in Europe, particularly in 1648 when the Holy Roman Empire was compelled to accept the signing of the treaty of Westphalia between Spain and the then named 'Republic of the Lowlands'. The signing of that treaty gave birth for the first time in history to what we now not only know but take for granted as the sovereign independent citizenship state where the power of the state is drawn from the power of the people at the bottom and then delegated upwards to the political levels (cf. Hāshim, 2018).

Before that, the right to rule was drawn either from on high, destined by Almighty God who was represented by the Pope or any similar deity according to the colour of faith, or by sheer power. However since the signing of the treaty of Westphalia, we have had for the first time in history the structurally secular state with territorially defined and recognized borders within which it enjoys sovereignty. Until then, the state, everywhere, was of the open-expansionary empire kind with no defined borders let alone recognized. After signing that treaty, the state began transforming so as to run smoothly in the grooves of the model of the secular citizen-based right to rule. Despotic monarchies began transforming into representative constitutional states until they have become symbolic and of nominal relevance. The treaty in fact brought about the demise of the Holy Roman Empire, giving way to a new Europe characterised by nation statehood and consequently paving the way for the dismantling of aristocracy and the feudal system which were rapidly replaced by the middle class of the bourgeois and capitalism. Liberalism (not necessarily democracy) was the convenient ideology of that new rising class. Along with that came a host of new innovations, such as industrialization, geographical explorations, slavery and later colonialism and apartheid etc (*ibid*).

Outside Europe, prior to colonialism, the institution of the state was still lagging behind. In some areas, such as China, Persia, Egypt and some other Arab places, the institution of the state was nationalized or rather grounded to variable degrees on a recognizable national identity. With the exception of Nubia and Abyssinia (present-day Sudan and Ethiopia respectively) sub-Saharan Africa did not know any national state. The state was still arrested in the ethnic boundary, not yet developed into any national dimension. There are many places in sub-Saharan Africa where the state was just one step from crossing the line to nationalism. However, before achieving this development, Western colonialism came into Africa. Those pre-national states of sub-Saharan Africa took the brunt of colonialism and were scrapped and relegated back into ethnic boundaries. In their place, the colonial powers of yesterday established a pseudo-national statehood that enjoyed recognizable borders but no real and actual sovereignty. The ethnic statehood nuclei along with their respective leaderships were kept arrested, forbidden from growing, and even turned into complicity.

Modern education, premised on reading and writing the languages of the colonial rule, was established to engender a pseudo-civil servant class and a pseudo-intellectual class at large. Thus education has become a tool for alienating the youngsters by luring them with the fake glory of the civil service jobs which were far well-paid than any other traditional profession no matter how anti-patriotic they were. That class of civil servants was actually countering the national public on behalf of their colonial masters.

In this way an anti-national state was erected by the colonial system where the civil service system at the bottom line was a lubricant to the colonial administrational machines that were stealing the wealth of the suppressed people of Africa. A similar anti-national institution with grave consequences was also built: that is the army which owned all the means and equipment of violence, legal or illegal. In its wake, the colonial imperialist Europe left Africa in a disarray, totally unprepared and unequipped to fill up the gap between the ethnic-bound state and the citizen-based state, no matter how an exemplar public service was left behind by he colonialist West. Good public service can help run a national state, but it cannot help making it.

Immediately after gaining their nominal independence, the armies, which were built by the colonial powers, ravaged and plundered savagely their African countries. Black Africans need to reconsider Nyerfere's not only bold and audacious but wise decision to dissolve the army inherited from the colonial systems of yesterday. Similarly, Amilcar Cabral (https://www.youtube.com/watch?v=rLo3Y2IG-iY), at the funeral of Nkrumah in 1972, questioned the national value of the colonial-built armies in Africa: "To what extent betrayal's success in Ghana linked to problems of class struggle, from contributions to social structure, from the role of party or other institutions including the armed forces as part of a new independent state. To what level, we should ask ourselves, is betrayal's success in Ghana linked to a correct definition of this historical entity and craftsman of history that is the people and their daily work, in defending its own independence conquest"?

This is what we Africans were left with when colonialism nominally left our African soil: we were left with no culture, no institution of governance. Our semi-national systems of governance were long since scrapped by colonialism. However, the ethnic groups, which were at the level of pre-national state were not only spared, but were further manipulated to the maximum by the colonial system. We were literally thrown off into the water while tied by all the robes and tangles of colonialism and at the same time we were supposed not to get wet.

3.8.1. Africa has to exhausting its Failure

In order to get free, it seems Africa must wreck itself and rid itself of anything it has benefitted from colonialism, whether it is political, cultural, institutional, or material. It seems it must exhaust its failure and get to the bottom-line so as to rise up again, free, developed and sovereign. This is very clear in the case of the post-apartheid African states. The challenge the African people of South Africa, Namibia, Zimbabwe are facing is how to get free from institutionalized apartheid without wrecking their respective countries. The argument goes as follows: Namibia tried not to go the same way Zimbabwe had taken. However, going that way seems inevitable if the deep structures of apartheid were meant to be dismantled. This is why the main trend in Pan Africanism has always refused to be part of the western propelled demonization of Robert Mugabe, without necessarily taking his side and condoning his mismanagement of the country and his dictatorship. After all who made him dictator other than Britain? Mugabe was their favourable boy as far as he kept the old system of apartheid intact. Zimbabwe for years kept winning agricultural awards as long as the produce was made by white people owned-farms to which the international markets were open. However, these markets were immediately closed when those farms were nationalized. Then the Anglo-American economic sanctions followed in order to bring Zimbabwe down to its knees but not until Britain and America were themselves exasperated. Now, the challenge for Namibia and South Africa is how to dismantle apartheid without wrecking their countries. The jury is out!.

CHAPTER 4

The Civil War and Aftermath
The Margin against the Centre

4.1. Introduction

The civil war in the Sudan began just one year before it achieved independence, i.e. in 1955. It would prove to be the longest civil war in the world as it kept going on for half a century with a brief interval of 10 years peace (1972 - 1983); it came to an end in 2005 and six years later the South became an independent state. Among a host of factors that played respective roles in staging the civil war, colonialism being one of them, one complex internal factor stands on its own as having the major role in the civil war, that is the structural racism deeply embedded in the psyche of the pseudo-Arabs of the Middle-North riverain Sudan against the marginalized black Africans of Sudan who had not yet been Arabized. It was part of the racism leveled by Arabized black Africans against their non-Arabized black African brethren, discussed in Chapter Two.

The split of the country between what was taken for granted to be the Muslim-Arab north and the pagan-Christian south was deeply rooted in the awareness of the middle-north riverain Sudanese elite. In 1953 the politicians of the middle-north riverain Sudan went to Egypt to attend the negotiation processes of the pre-independence administration that were held by the condominium rule partners, Britain and Egypt. Not a single Southerner was included in that delegation. The Southerners were very disappointed and voiced their dissatisfaction. Some say that at the time there was no Southern party to participate. However, this shows the ideological split to the extent that each of the two parts of the country were supposed to have their respective political parties. In the 1954 elections of the self-rule parliament, the Southerners managed to represent themselves with one-third of the total number of representatives. This also marks the moment when the middle-north riverain elites began politically encroaching into the South, and attracting members into their Northern parties. The ballot weight of the South was to be manipulated by the political parties of the North for their own benefit.

The policy of Sudanization was adopted in 1954 whereby key governmental posts were to be filled by Sudanese. At the dawn of independence, as the colonial condominium rule began preparing to take its leave, the capability of the Sudanese elite class was at stake. The question was whether the Sudanese elite would prove itself capable of running the country, capitalizing on the relative advancement realized during the colonial rule, while keeping the unity of the nation intact and prosperous. However, to the disappointment of all observers, the middle-north riverain Sudanese intellectuals and politicians not only failed to win the hearts of their southern brethren but further widened the mistrust.

In response to the vocal protestations of the Southerners, Khartoum had no sense except the threat of heavy-handed retaliation, a matter that widened the gap of mistrust more than ever. In line with the mistrust of Khartoum, the authorities empowering the civil administrators were transferred to the police thus marginalizing the former who had run the South for decades. All this gave birth to the call of the South to have a confederal relationship with the North, a matter that was flatly rejected by the middle-north riverain elites. Defiantly, many of the Southern intellectuals went to the extreme and began demanding separation.

The pseudo-Arab Sudanese intellectual class was so shortsighted and incapacitated and completely encapsulated in its tiny ideological shell of arrogance and resentment of everything African to the extent that it seemed as though it had never dawned on them that their country could not be confined to the Arabized middle-north riverain Sudan. Taking the Southerners and all black non-Arabized Africans of the Sudan for granted, they began filling the vacant jobs with people not only belonging to the Islamo-Arab ideology, but with those who belonged to their very small and closed clique of friends, relations, and school friends etc. The job share of the Southerners was very meagre when compared with that of the Northerners. From that time, the mentality of the Northerners when redressing the grievances they inflicted on the Southerners in any peace-seeking negotiations would be conditioned by that job offers. Later, when other marginalized people in parts other than the South (such as Darfur, Kordufan, the East, and the Blue Nile etc) took to arms, the conditioned mentality of that job-offer would prove to be time-resistant and too hard to change.

Rather than to wake up and try to amend their wrongdoings, they tended to consolidate their closed apartheid-like power circles every time the Southerners expressed their dismay at what was going on. Furthermore, lest the Southerners take any measure against the policy of Sudanization, and out of sheer mistrust, they began deploying the military battalions and divisions stationed in the South, the majority of whose soldiers were from the South, to various areas in the north so as to scatter them.

In 1955, one year before independence, the civil war took off in the South, led by what came to be known as the '*Anya-Nya*' movement. Enough was enough! It kept going on and on until the South pulled out in 2011 as a direct result of the foolish, good-for-nothing and adamant mentality of the middle-north riverain Sudanese politicians, intellectuals and people at large. Many trials and attempts were made to bring about lasting peace but in vain. In 1972 the Addis Ababa Accord was signed, only to be abrogated by Khartoum in 1983. How sustainable peace could be achieved when the only card the middle-north riverain Sudanese politicians had was their conditional job-offer, with no space or prospect of addressing the historic grievances!

4.2. On the Epistemology of Civil Wars in the Sudan

Civil wars can be classified in many ways according to the context in which the concerned civil wars take place and according to the perspectives and assumptions adopted. In the Sudan, at least, two kinds of civil wars can be observed. The first is what we call the "leverage war", which is launched in order to pressurize the central government so as to make it respond positively to certain demands. The Southern Sudanese *Anya-Nya* civil war (1955 - 1973) fits into this class as it was directly triggered, among other indirect factors of influence, by the policy of Sudanization by which senior government posts were being filled by Northern Sudanese at the time of the departure of the British administration. Understandably, the Addis Ababa Accord that brought that 17 year war to an end was typically post-based, as it granted the Southerners posts that ranged from bottom to top echelon levels. In any leverage war, the central government is primarily responsible for instigating the war and consequently, primarily responsible to bring it to an end. Civil wars take place as a necessity and not as a choice, as civilians would only go into an armed rebellion against their government as a last resort. This is why the central government stands responsible for having a national group launching a war against it. In such civil wars, negotiation is the best means through which the central government can bring the rebel group into peace. The best negotiations are initiated by the central government with convincing offers and delegations from each party working towards reaching a successful peace agreement. In cases where no such offer is forthcoming, intervention from outside is likely to take place. The outsiders usually come with their own agenda but not before having leverage on both warring sides. History has shown us that in such cases the peace reached is usually at the expense of the rebel groups.

Whatever the situation, it is worth mentioning that both this kind of civil war and peace negotiation are linear, not holistic (comprehensive), with only two alternatives: either continued war or a limited sense of peace. Therefore negotiation will never bring about any lasting solution for the war. It will just be an episode of disengagement.

The second class of wars is what we call the "liberation war", which is launched to overhaul the whole system in order to introduce a new system in its place. This is the revolutionary approach to achieve radical national change; it must be based on the aspirations of a vast number of people whose awareness rising becomes one of the prime targets of the revolutionary organization. This kind of war is circular as it is holistic and aims at bringing about radical changes. The war launched by the late Dr. John Garang de Mabior under the banner of "Sudan People Liberation Movement / Army" (SPLM/A) in 1983 fits into this classification. The notion of "liberation war" itself is drawn by the present author from its experience. And this shows how far-sighted and visionary Garang was in naming the movement he launched a liberating one. In such wars, no negotiation can stop the war other than negotiating the guarantees offered by the revolutionary party to the leaders of the central government with regards to either their safety or a safe exit from the country. This is why the central governments do their best to transform the liberation war into leverage war, i.e. the one that can have its demands met through negotiations, i.e. to transform it from being a circular war into a linear war that can be settled through a linear negotiation. Once this takes place it means the abortion of the revolutionary nature of the liberating organization. In such cases, usually outside intervention is the main initiator of negotiation as it has leverage on both fighting parties. No lasting peace can come out of such negotiations, as the compelling factors that had instigated the civil war fundamentally remain unanswered. Understandably the privileged party in these kinds of peace negotiations is the central government as it is taken on board as a partner rather than facing the revolutionary end of expulsion.

The Naivacha peace negotiations between the SPLM/A and the Islamo-Arab regime of Khartoum under pressure from the USA and Britain is an example of this kind of negotiation, by which the revolutionary nature of the SPLM/A is liquidated. A circular revolutionary organization was compelled to transform into a linear one. Understandably the Comprehensive Peace Agreement (CPA) signed in 2005 was a linear one. The liquidation of the revolutionary nature of the SPLM/A has proved to be very catastrophic for the Sudan, which was a united country now divided into two states: North Sudan and South Sudan. The corrupt and failed regime in North Sudan is still in office, while another typical corrupt and failed regime is instated in South Sudan with civil wars raging in both parts of the country. Then why the negotiations and why all the Hubbub and hullabaloo?

4.3. SPLM/SPLA

In 1983 a group of Southern military soldiers rebelled and took to the jungle: the second phase of the civil war had begun. It would prove to be the longest civil war in modern history, claiming the lives of millions of Southern civilians who perished unnoticed either at the hands of the marauding government army or caught in the crossfire.

The rebellion was engineered by three different groups and was very soon joined by veterans of the first phase civil war. The scenario of civilian tragedies and the legacy of that war with its demand for the separation of Southern Sudan loomed up in the minds of the Sudanese people. Of the three factions that were behind the rebellion, at least one of them was wholly committed to the separation of the South, formed mainly of remnants of the Anya-Nya who refused to accept the Addis Ababa Accord (Johnson, 2003). Then, a highly educated senior army officer, who was also a veteran of the first civil war, joined the rebellion to emerge as its paramount military commander and intellectual thinker.

This was Dr. Col. John Garang de Mabior, who made Sudan take its sharpest turn in history since the establishment of the Funj Sultanate in 1505: the unification of the marginal forces against the centre.

The rebellious body was called "the Sudan People Liberation Movement" (SPLM) with its military arm called "the Sudan People Liberation Army" (SPLA). Although greatly and understandably overshadowed by the South, the movement declared in its manifesto that it was concerned with the whole Sudan. It also stated that the war was not a war of the South against the North, but rather it was the war of marginalized people in the South, the Upper Blue Nile, the Nuba Mountains, the West, the East and the North against the centre which is represented by the government of Khartoum and its entourage of elites, which is not in any way the true government of the whole Sudan. The dominance of the centre and its exploitation of the marginalized people was so deeply rooted in the system that only an armed liberation movement could undo it, that is to say to transcend the linear polarization model (South vs. North) to the circular polarization model (margin vs. centre); and to say to transcend the melting pot model of nationalism to the unity in diversity model of nationalism. The true version of Afro-Arabism as the identity of Sudan was declared where the plural components of Africanism and Arabism should be honoured on an equal footing without violating the rights of any party. All this was concluded under the banner of the "New Sudan". Its manifesto also criticized the Addis Ababa Accord, pointing to the tricky tactic of job-offer.

While calling people from marginalized areas to join the liberation movement, it also called intelligent people who belong to the Arabic-oriented middle Sudan to join. All people of Sudan, whether in the middle or periphery, needed to liberate themselves from the vicious entanglement of centro-marginalization. The process of centro-marginalization victimizes the Sudanese Muslims in general, and the Sudanese Arabs in particular, by creating the false impression that it works in their interest.

It took Sudan five centuries to reach this point of national maturity. The assimilation and melting pot model of nationalism inaugurated by ʿAbdu Allah Jammāʿ and ʿAmāra Dungus had served Sudan well in the aftermath of the fall of the Christian Kingdoms. For four centuries, it had been working to that effect until the Mahdia revolution. Since then it has outlived its virtues. In one century Sudan has made huge leaps toward national maturity. The Mahdia revolution, under the leadership of al-Mahdi, emerged as a peoples revolt representing the margin, crumbled under the weight of the central state of the Mahdi's successor, al-Khalīfa ʿAbdu Allāhī. Later, standing against the British-Egyptian colonial rule, the farsighted visions of ʿAlī ʿAbdu al-Laṭīf in theory and practice were hatched only to be aborted by the system of the middle-north riverain prestigma that allied itself with the British colonial rule.

The honourable life and death of the martyr Maḥmūd Muḥammad Ṭāha symbolizes the sacrificial readiness and nobility of the Sudanese people. Furthermore, he demonstrated how thought is much stronger than arms, and how thought defeats death. His life is a series of lessons on how misgovernment (and fanaticism) can be fought and defeated by a constant civilian attitude. This goes in line with the attitude of the Sudanese people in regard to public uprisings and revolts against dictatorship. Both the revolutions of October 1964 and April 1985 stand as great examples for us to follow. Ṭāha's noble way of dying is also a lesson on how to stand firm and die – peacefully like Socrates – sticking to one's cause and beliefs rather than to compromise them.

As a sequential resultant of all these developments came the movement led by John Garang de Mabior, particularly with respect to its thought and deeds, i.e. praxis. Those are the pillars of Sudanese nationalism. By then, the core theoretical homework had already been done by the Sudanese intellectuals who fought bravely their way through racial bigotry and religious fanaticism, from subjective to objective reasoning. In fact, every Sudanese intellectual - regardless of being pro or contra - is honoured by virtually being engaged in the argument in concern. It started from the level of the melting pot and steadily developed to the level of unity in diversity, from assimilation to integration.

4.4. The Emergence of the Sudanese Middle

At the beginning, very few people took the words of the SPLM/SPLA seriously. The people from the margin began taking the movement at its word slowly. After so many centuries of subjugation and intimidation, it was so difficult for them to believe in freedom at its face value. Then they began adhering to the movement. The people of the margin joined the call of the movement in accordance with their degree of stigma: the more stigmatized the people, the more enthusiastic they were in taking to arms (‹1› the South, ‹2› Blue Nile and Nuba Mountains, ‹3› the West, ‹4› the East and ‹5› last, but not least, the North). A considerable number of people who were socially supposed to belong to the prestigma showed their national far-sightedness by joining the movement as soldiers and politicians.

Being the most stigmatized, the Southerners were the core of the movement and its army. As was the case in the first civil war, they took it also to be their own war. This made the movement accommodate the separatist trends but only covertly. The national nature of the movement did not dawn on them until later when supporters from outside the South began appearing among their ranks. Given the relatively small number of these supporters, the national dimension of the movement was not immediately felt in a direct way. It was extremely distressing for the Southerners to fight and die on behalf of other people who did not support them even sentimentally, to say nothing of the *mondukuru*. Nevertheless, they kept fighting under the banner of liberating the whole of Sudan. The increased numbers of people joining the movement, with whole areas (such as areas of 2nd and 3rd degrees of stigma) taking to arms, soothed their hurt feelings and boosted their morale.

By declining separatism and declaring that the fight was for the whole of the Sudan, the margin achieved a high level of awareness, maturity and bravery. It came to discern the truth that the so-called Sudan was the historical homeland of the Africans. If the Arabs came to live with them, they would be welcome; there was enough room for everybody. But if the Arabs came to be masters of the land and to relegate the Africans to second place, then they would have to fight for it. It was a historic moment that saw the subsequent birth of the Sudanese Middle. Coming from the columns of the political left, they were, truly speaking, the left-middle or the Sudano-African middle.

But where is the right-middle or the Sudano-Arab middle? Its maturity depends on the intelligence and transparency of the enlightened groups who have been brought up socially as belonging to the prestigma and the centre, whether they are from the middle of Sudan or from its periphery. They need to discover that they belong to the truly honourable Arab culture and Islam, not to the prestigma or the centre. Sudan will become a mature democracy only if the adherents of this political middle have developed a progressive national consciousness of true Afro-Arabism.

Three movements that appeared among the university students and the intellectual sectors respectively are believed by the present writer to belong to the right-middle or Sudano-Arab Middle, namely the Congress of Independent Students (CIS), the Movement of Neutral Students (MNS), and the Movement of the New Democratic Forces (known as *ḤAQ*, as a partial acronym in Arabic). Each will be reviewed shortly below.

The movement of the Congress of Independent Students could have been the true launch of the Sudano-Arab middle with wide arms to embrace Sudano-African dimensions as well, were it not for its incapable and crippled organizational body. Although the Southern students did not contribute to its making as they had had their own political organization, the movement was supported however in its early days by students from all parts of the Sudan. Contrary to the idea it advocated, the strong winds of prestigma blew the sails of the movement. Gradually students from marginalized areas dropped out; it was very awkward for them with their 'twisted tongues' (indicating not mastering Arabic) to remain with people who spoke the highly idiomatic colloquial Arabic of middle Sudan. On the other hand, it was also awkward for other students to talk in the presence of marginalized students about racial discrimination or cultural persecution, something they never suffered from themselves. It was a situation where the marginalized students were better placed in matters pertaining to leadership. Furthermore, with the intensification of marginalization, students from marginalized areas withdrew deep into their ethnic boundaries. The marginalized groups did not yet identify with each other, let alone with enlightened people from the centre. By the late 1990s, with the rise of the intellectual discourse of the movement, the organized body shrank to a countable number of students, most of whom came from prestigmatic backgrounds.

The large numbers of the graduates of the CIS have remained organizationally inactive, as they do not have any body to join. The majority of this group is politically active on an intellectual basis, which is likely to materialize in a kind of political body at any moment. The remaining are divided between two political organizations, namely a civilian political party established in 1986, and an armed opposition organization established in 1994. The former (the National Congress Party - NCP) did not fare well during the democratic period to the extent that the present military Islamo-Arabist regime vindictively usurped the name when it decided to have its own political party. All this time the National Congress Party (Opposition) - as it distinguished itself then - has consumed whatever energy it has in this futile battle of regaining its name. Presently it has adopted the name of Sudanese Congress Party. The armed organization (Sudan Allied Forces - SAF) came into existence by timidly admitting its commitment in a way to the Islamic and Arabic culture of the middle Sudan. This is the reason for its failure to join SPLM/SPLA from the beginning, which it did not bother to explain [Hāshim, 1999b]. Lately a merger with SPLM/SPLA was negotiated, to be temporarily aborted by internal dissension as well as external factors pertaining to the process of peace negotiations in Naivasha, Kenya. The move to drop the Nuba Mountains and Blue Nile from the agenda and confining the peace accord within the frontiers of the South was a move deemed too complicated.

The movement of the Congress of Independent Students (CIS) has so far exerted relentless efforts to muster its dispersed forces and potential members without tangible results. Since 1979, thousands and thousands of members of this movement have graduated from their respective universities inside and outside Sudan. With no inclusive political body to uphold them, they have amazingly kept the fire kindled and ablaze in their hearts. While the two political organizations that emerged from this movement (the NCP and the SAF) have not succeeded in recruiting those graduates, no other political party can claim to have attracted them into its ranks. The reason behind this is that those people can only be politically organized to the accompaniment of their distinguished intellectual discourse of cultural analysis and the theory of margin vs. centre of which they are very proud, something both the NCP and the SAF have dismissed out of miscalculated pragmatism.

The shrinkage of the Congress of Independent Students by early 1990s in the universities and higher educational institutions led to the emergence of another identical movement called the Movement of Neutral Students (MNS). Naturally, the University of Khartoum witnessed the birth of this movement. Initiated and led mostly by frustrated members of the CIS, it understandably raised the same banners of Sudanese nationalism and democracy, but not the African identity of the Sudan, or the struggle to dismantle the institution of marginalization. Like its predecessor, it also promised not to deviate from the righteous mission of voicing the needs of the students instead of using them for political ends.

In 1991 it succeeded in achieving a sweeping victory in the elections of Khartoum University Students Union (KUSU) against a coalition representing the National Democratic Alliance, which was the main opposition movement, and the Islamic National Movement, which was toppled from the KUSU despite the fact that it was backed by the junta regime. Soon after that, the movement spread to other universities. However, the infant movement crumbled under the oppressive and intimidating measures taken against it by the regime. In 1993, the security organs of the regime stormed the university precinct, chased the students through the university precincts where it fatally shot three students and mass-arrested the leading figures of the MNS who were members of the KUSU at the same time. Eventually, the university was closed and the KUSU was dismantled. That was the beginning of the shrinking of the movement as an organized body. However, it has kept going on and on as a loose and diminishing movement just as the CIS has done. By the mid-1990s, many of the leading figures of the MNS who had graduated showed up among the ranks of the SAF. So far most of its affiliates are still out there without a shepherding organization that can make them play their destined role in Sudanese history.

By the mid-1990s two events took their toll on a large number of Sudanese intellectuals who belonged to the classic Left, namely the disintegration of the Soviet Union and the Iraqi invasion of Kuwait. The first disillusioned a large number of the socialist and Communist sector; the second frustrated an equal number of the Sudanese Pan-Arabists. That was the season of discontent of the Sudanese Socialist intellectuals, as a wave of frustration swept across them. In 1994, a group of Sudanese intellectuals in exile engaged themselves in heated discussions regarding the deteriorating conditions of the Sudan. Large numbers of the socialist drop-outs joined them. Those discussions led to the formation of the Democratic Forum, which was based in London, UK, with many branches in various western countries.

By 1995, the hectic activities of the Democratic Forum culminated in the formation of the Movement of the New Democratic Forces (known as *ḤAQ*). Then, a high-profile intellectual bravely announced his breakaway from the Sudanese Communist Party where he had enjoyed the membership of its Central Committee and played a crucial role in founding *ḤAQ*. That was al-Khātim ʽAdlān, a top leader of the Communist and socialist students in Khartoum University in the late 1960s and early 1970s, and who passed away prematurely in April 2005 in London (1/1/1948 - 23/4/2005). *ḤAQ* was soon acclaimed as a true substitute for the ailing and old political parties, left or right alike. With the same speed, it began spreading in Sudanese universities, mostly to the detriment of both the CIS and the MNS as it also raised the same banners of democracy, peace, fighting marginalization and reconsidering the African component of the Sudanese identity. However, *ḤAQ* did not achieve any significant progress because it consumed most of its energy rivaling other political organizations, and as it had also been hampered by the political and ideological legacies of its founders and leaders, indulging itself in successive breakaways and split-ups.

It was deemed crucially improtant in Sudanese history that such movements (particularly those mentioned above) managed to develop into a kind of inclusive political coalition. The Left-Middle could not do the job alone as one palm does not clap. It can easily be targeted by Islamo-Arabism as an anti-Islamic, anti-Arab movement, as it really includes non-Muslim and non-Arab people. Such accusations can hardly be leveled on the right-middle, which is mostly Muslim and Arabized. However, nothing was forthcoming in this regard.

Presently, only the CIS is active in Sudanese universities and enjoying a crystal clear national discourse based on the cultural analysis and the call for the dismantlement of the centre and empowering the marginalized people. However, it is hampered and ill-fated by being affiliated to a party of strong prestigmatic and Islamo-Arab tendencies (the Sudanese Congress party). Whether CIS will manage to *liberate* itself from this pretsigmatic bondage or not remains an open question. Bearing the cross of stigma on their back for so long made it very natural for marginalized people to fight against the prestigma for freedom, justice, and peace. But to fight against the prestigma with the aim of dismantling it and reinstating in its place a new Sudan based on the principles of freedom, justice, and peace, while coming from a prestigmatised background, is a great mission that can only be shouldered by a great people. The stalemate still goes on.

4.5. The undoing of the Stigma: the South leading the Sudan

As expected, the establishment of the prestigma took the declaration of the SPLM/SPLA to liberate the Sudan lightly at first. When the seriousness of the movement was made clearly and practically tangible, then the prestigma gave vent to its venom: it took it as appallingly repulsive for the slaves to boast of freeing their masters. Sarcastic and bitter jokes were cracked, picturing John Garang having at his food table the prestigious girls and women of the centre as servants handing him food and drinks. The joke lies in reversing the picture of the prestigmatic slaver. The machine of stigma/prestigma was never in such frenzy.

By the turn of the century, with the semi-circle of the civil war spreading to the West, Nuba Mountains, the South, Blue Nile and the East, the movement succeeded in securing the allegiance and moral support of the people of the circular margin, i.e. including the Nubians in the North who were the last to join and the least likely to take to arms. By this time the movement had fought against three political regimes: two military dictatorships and an elected government in between, with the programme of mono-culturalism, Arabicization and centro-marginalization shared in common by all three. From this point of view, as far as the movement was concerned, there was no difference whether the ruling system was totalitarian or democratic. The ideological parameters for both were the same.

During the dictatorship of the May regime, the opposition parties of the centre had allied covertly with the movement, applauding its military victories out of vindictiveness toward the regime. By the fall of the May regime and the restoration of democracy, the majority of the centre thought that there was no reason for the SPLM/SPLA to fight; they sincerely waited and then urged John Garang to put down arms and join the peaceful democratic process. That was because they did not take him seriously right from the beginning. They thought that he was just imitating them when he used the word "liberation", playing with words while his ultimate goal was to have the May regime toppled so he could be a minister, or even a prime minister. It took them the period of democratic rule to come to the realization that the man was deadly serious, but not before cursing him enough.

By the coming of the present military regime in 1989, the opposition parties of the centre overtly declared their alliance with the SPLM/SPLA. They did this without bothering to exercise any self-criticism, especially the parties that formed the government that escalated the war in the first place. Shortly before the coup, a group of intellectuals venturing an attempt to broker peace talks contacted John Garang. Immediately on their return, they were put in prison upon orders from the Minister of the Interior, Mubārak al-Fāḍil al-Mahdi (of Umma party). Days after the military coup, the same minister slipped out of the country and braced himself for fighting the junta by joining the military opposition led by the same John Garang. The farce went to its limit when the junta freed the very intellectuals imprisoned by the same former minister.

Although civilian by nature, the political opposition parties – out of total ineptitude – fled their civilian battlefield, which was within the country, and feigned a boastful military posture. With a fake epaulette, they joined the SPLM/SPLA in the armed struggle to topple the military regime. Part of their plan was to co-opt the movement by assimilating it into a bigger body. All in all, the stratagem was that they would take over the political leadership and leave the movement to do the military job, i.e. the fighting. The master thinks of what to grow, but it is the slave who toils and cultivates the land. This time they got it wrong.

The only positive thing that resulted from that alliance was the normalization of the nation-wide leadership of John Garang. This normalization effectively countered the stigmatic image painted by the machine of the prestigma, which was getting agitated. Both vices (i.e. prestigma and stigma) were conjoined like Siamese twins - undoing either one of them consequently resulted in the dismantling of the other.

4.6. Garang vs. al-Turābi: a Comparison of Leadership

For the last five centuries, i.e. since the establishment of the Black Sultanate, the process of centro-marginalization as based on the linear polarization has been going on. It was John Garang who launched the era of common awareness of anti-marginalization and who brought to the public stage the awareness of circular polarization. Although his vision was not based on theorization, it was however made very simple in short idiomatic phrases and slogans, like pressing buttons; once pressed a whole programme will open up. His crystal clear vision of nationalism as enshrined in his programme for the New Sudan would shape the future of the marginalized people of Sudan. To the present writer, to keep silent about his noble struggle and his fighting against the centre, which has been an example to be followed by other marginalized groups all over the Sudan, would amount to nothing short of treason.

Against the picture of John Garang drawn above and the growing image of his national leadership, it would be good to make a comparison with a high-profile political leader from the Islamo-Arab centre that is Ḥasan al-Turābi, the leader of the so-called Islamic Movement in the Sudan. Al-Turābi, in his vigorous pursuit to fulfil his obsessive dream of becoming the Head of State, led the movement of the Muslim Brothers for almost four decades (1960-2000) only to attain power by a military coup. During the third democracy (1985-1989) his party (the National Islamic Front - NIF), being the real opposition, had been one step from winning the next election if it had not joined the failing government of al-Ṣādig al-Mahdi in 1988, then named the government of *al-wifāq*, i.e. concordance. No reason can be discerned for that fatal and uncalculated move of joining that failing government, other than al-Turābi's whimsical and uncontrollable drive for power. By becoming part of the executive body, the ineptitude of the NIF was exposed overnight. The fact that the movement of Muslim Brothers relied ultimately on slogans without having any applicable programme was dawning on the ordinary people who had previously fallen prey to its Islamic slogans. This took a great toll on the popularity of the NIF as the masses became disillusioned. Months later, i.e. in 1989, the government of *al-wifāq* collapsed and was replaced by a national government also led by al-Ṣādig al-Mahdi. That was the moment when the NIF decided to topple the chronically ailing democratic government using its military recruits in the army who had been prepared for the mission a long time before, even before the fall of Nimeiri's regime.

On June 30, 1989 the NIF's coup took place. By the evening of that day it became common knowledge that it was the NIF that was behind the coup. However, the NIF vehemently denied that, especially al-Turābi who was arrested along with the political figures of the democratic era. No one believed him, however, as the coup represented what was typical of him. Known as a political chameleon, he had changed the name and colour of his political party five times in five decades (1960 - 2010). All this could have been counted to his credit, if all that was not attributed to his known opportunism and spinelessness, if not sheer cowardice. Not sure that the coup could hold on, al-Turābi allowed the junta to rule while constantly denying that the coup had any links with the NIF. Right from the beginning, some inconspicuous figures of the third echelon of the NIF showed up among the ranks of the junta, to be followed by relatively prominent figures from the second echelon in 1990. By 1992, conspicuous figures from the first echelon, such as ʿAlī ʿUthmān Muḥammad Ṭāha (al-Turābi's deputy in the NIF) timidly showed their faces only to immediately lose their bashfulness. Until now al-Turābi had not shown up. Only in 1996, i.e. seven years after the coup had taken place, did he dare show his face as an original player in the game of power and rule. He came to the theatre of power assuming that his seat of leadership was reserved for him. By then the pawns, who were supposed to be ruling by proxy for the leader in hiding, had developed a taste for the power to which they had got too accustomed. As they were aware of the crucial role they played in consolidating the rule of their unpopular coup, they were also well aware of the real reasons behind al-Turābi's hiding for so long. The irony was that when al-Turābi thought that he was very close to fulfilling his dream, he discovered that he was farther away from it than ever.

That was enough to drive him to a frenzy and he revolted against President ʿUmar al-Bashīr to the extent of threatening to join the SPLM/SPLA, as if the latter could have accepted him. Shamelessly, the breakaway faction (of Ḥasan al-Turābi) joined the club of opposition raising high the banner of democracy: the same democracy that they conspired to kill. Counting on the forgetfulness of the people, it did not bother to display the slightest self-criticism that could grant them self-respect. Armed with a huge amount of money they had appropriated from the state resources and tax revenues, they made their cynical show among the ranks of the opposition, led then by the SPLM/SPLA. Of course that move added to the normalization of the national image of the leader of SPLM/SPLA, John Garang. However, al-Turābi by then had exhausted all his wits and plots. Having reached his eighties, he was running out of time with a bitter taste of salt in his mouth. Al-Turābi was like the wizard that was bitten by his own poisonous snake.

On March 5, 2016 al-Turābi passed away in Khartoum at the age of 84 most of which was wasted in political witchery. ʿUmar Ḥasan al-Bashīr may not be only the worst Sudanese president ever; he may truly prove to be the worst among those yet to come. However, the only person worse than al-Bashīr is definitely al-Turābi who had cynically picked him out of many military officers nominated to lead the coup.

Moaning under the yoke of the Muslim Brothers, the Sudanese people could only look with hope to John Garang. After all, he was the only one who stood firmly against the dictatorial Islamic regime, inflicting defeat after defeat upon them. The Muslim Brothers came with the aim of annihilating his army, but that war ended by his liberating the whole South and giving it its own flag and its own coin and various public utilities. The Muslim Brothers, on the other hand, ended with dissension and split up. The first reaction of the head thinker, i.e. Ḥasan al-Turābi who combined both fanaticism and pragmatism, was to join John Garang, whereas the head ruler, i.e. President ʿUmar Ḥasan al-Bashīr (with frowning anti-charismatic image), pretended to cling to the gun while retreating. This situation kept on reversing occasionally. Neither the former nor the latter was sincere about peace; they were instead keen on settling accounts of personal vendettas regarding leadership and the presidency. They were like the two car thieves who are quarrelling at the steering wheel while driving the stolen car. This is the natural fruition of ideological stupidity and religious fanatical insanity.

As all this may show the growing national image of the SPLM/SPLA leader, John Garang, it also shows the contradictions of the situation in Sudan. The enemies of yesteryear become friends of today, only to resume their enmity tomorrow, and vice-versa. This polarization does not seem to result from firm ideological stands, but rather from vindictive opportunism and political buffoonery. On the other side, this seems to be firmly rooted in the ideology of prestigma/stigma, centre/margin as factions that historically belong to the prestigma are ready to go to any ends in their quest for power, and desire to subjugate the margin/stigma. Sudan has never been in such a precarious situation. Something should be done ... this madness should be stopped and a lasting peace must be achieved. But how? The crucial question is how can Sudan achieve a lasting and comprehensive peace without disintegrating? Such a peace would boost the national image of John Garang and consequently put the Southerners in the front lines of national politics and leadership. Along with the Southerners, other marginalized people will come forward to assume their rightful place in the national arena. The prestigma will never allow this to happen.

4.7. The Desperado Prestigma is selling out the Sudan

Never has the prestigma been faced with such a problem in its long history. There is only one way left in order to get out of this dilemma half victorious: to strip this John Garang De Mabior of the ability to be a national leader and reduce him to a Southerner once again, then to make him an offer that he cannot decline without bringing about his own demise. The deal is going to cost the Sudan the loss of the whole South. This will give the prestigma an injection of life by simply keeping other degrees of stigma tethered a little longer to the prestigmatic centre. To do this successfully they need the ethically unrestricted force of a superpower – America's think-tank is always ready for such missions, and this time the old British Empire came behind with its colonial expertise like an old grandmother behind her big grandson.

When the war kept going on and on without any prospect of solution, the Southerners began losing faith in the nationalist approach of the SPLM/SPLA. By 1990, the war reached an extreme degree of intensification. The government fought it as an Islamic *jihad*, a matter that has alienated the Southerners more than ever. People and villages were razed to the ground under the marauding advance of the *jihadist* armies and militias. A human being standing on earth claimed no more dignity than a shriveled tree. The Southerners outside the war zone, especially in exile, could stand that no longer. The call for separating the South was once again revived. The retreat of the Southerners from the ranks of the left-middle to the ranks of the separatist Left began. It took them two decades of betrayal and frustration, from 1972-1993, to reach this point. Meanwhile, the extreme Right never abandoned the idea and possibility of separating the South. The junta in their early days in 1989 made that offer, but backed down under strong public condemnation. It was also declined by the SPLM/SPLA as was expected according to its nationalist banners, i.e. by being Left-middle. This time the institution of prestigma tacitly endorsed the call for separation made then by some Southern intellectuals. America and Britain dashed onto the scene when they smelt oil. The scenario of the peace initiative of Naivacha then brokered was put forward.

With the prospects of Sudan becoming an oil country it is only a matter of time until America pushes its way with heavy-handed diplomacy. It is like a splash of blood in the Red Sea; sharks will immediately smell it. And after all, it was Chevron, an American company, which discovered that oil in the first place, before selling out the concession. More opportunely, the richest fields are in the South, where, fortunately for the Americans, there is a civil war against a dictatorial regime. A dictatorial regime is the best thing America can dream of for a third world country. If it accepts the manipulating friendship of America, then long life is guaranteed to the dictatorship; if it does not, nothing is easier and more ethically acceptable for the biggest democracy in the world than to target a third world dictatorship. The West in general and America in particular, seem to hate nothing more than seeing democracy flourish in the third world.

Separating the South will leave the North in its status quo where the privileged ruling class, i.e. the prestigma will keep on going. Adopting the battered Islamic regime of Sudan will not only do that, but will also let the Americans put their hands on virgin fields rich with oil. In the independent state of what has become the South Sudan, a despotic government is understandably the kind of rule America will support. An interim period is vitally important so as the central government in Khartoum can generously give the Americans firm foot ground in the South that cannot be repealed by the later independent Southern government. Furthermore, a repentant Islamic fundamentalist government in the Northern state of Sudan is needed by the Americans to accomplish another job (currently Libya and Iraq respectively provide good examples of how a prodigal revolutionist, like Muammar Gaddafi, can prove to be more compliant to America than transplanting a puppet ruler, like Eyad Allawi). Instead of reconsidering their policies towards the Muslims, the Americans are unwittingly trying hard to bring the Islamic fundamentalist movements back under harness. A new kind of well-domesticated Islamic fundamentalism remotely controlled by America – not like the one that went wildly out of control in Afghanistan

– is needed and is possible to be engineered. This is how America is going to reconcile itself with Islam, by robbing and subjugating Muslims. And this is how America is going to support black Africa, by robbing and subjugating Africans. America is might, but with no equal wisdom.

In the past, America was not very interested in the Sudan as it was considered to be one of the poorest countries in the world. Now, realising the huge resources Sudan possesses in oil, America will do anything but help this giant to rise up. This is our time, we the Sudanese people, to prove to the Third World that the battle against the unwise administrations of America can be won without war, by civilization, (i.e. by adopting the ways and means of Maḥmūd Muḥammad Ṭāha) which can only be realized by making freedom, justice, and peace prevail in the Sudan in particular and in African and the Third World in general.

4.8. A Circular Civil War but a Linear Peace

By claiming that it came to liberate Sudan from the hegemony of the centre, which relegates the whole country into marginalization, especially the periphery, SPLM/SPLA became very attractive to people from the margin. It included among its fighters people from the Nuba Mountains, Blue Nile, Beja, Darfur and representative figures from all over the country. At present, the civil war is not only in the South; it has spread to these other parts of the margin. The war has almost become circular, i.e. it can only be described in terms of the margin vs. the centre. If there is any peace to be brokered, it should be inclusive in respect of all marginalized groups fighting alongside the SPLM/SPLA. However, the peace initiative which was brokered mainly by America, Britain, Norway and other western countries and which was signed in 2005 between the government and the SPLM/SPLA, was concerned only with the civil war in the South. Like the rest of the West, America and Britain have persistently decided to deal with the civil war in Sudan as between the black African and Christian South against the Muslim and Arab North.

There is no sense in putting out the fire in part of the house while other parts are aflame. There is no sense in deciding to put an end to the war in the South while leaving it to flare up in the Blue Nile, Darfur, the Nuba Mountains or the Beja, especially when the causes of the war are the same and the fighting groups have achieved a kind of unifying vision and body. It just does not make sense! Something is suspect here. It is much easier to deal with a single body which can help settle the whole conflict in one stroke rather than to have many parties to deal with. What is the wisdom behind telling the other parties to wait until the fight in the South comes to an end? It is like telling them to keep on fighting until you reach a deal with the biggest fighting group. Is it that they have not yet claimed enough importance, or that the wars they are engaged in have not yet claimed enough lives?

The way to rationalize this approach is to assume that the war is between the South and the North, a matter that will take us back to the stereotype of Arab-Muslim North vs. Christian-African South, i.e. the linear polarization with its concept of centro-marginalization, cultural reproduction and the whole system of stigma/prestigma. One can expect such a peace to be brokered by the institution of the prestigma only. But this peace is being brokered by America and Britain! Even the Western mass media and academia, generally speaking, stubbornly stick to the linear polarization. Is it simply complicity, or the shortsightedness of stereotype? How can the fighters of Nuba Mountains, The Blue Nile, the Beja and Darfur be disengaged from the fight led by the SPLM/SPLA? The sophisticated answer is because they are Northerners. But what about the Dinka of Southern Kordufan? The linear shallowness, which is accommodated simply because of complicity, shows in the answer that boundaries can be adjusted a little to include them in the South. If this is possible, why not adjust it a little further to include, for instance, the Nuba Mountains fighters as they are also from Southern Kordufan? Why not push the line a little northward to include the Funj, Uduk, Ingassena, Berti, and Hamaj etc? This seems to be a Byzantine argument, simply because of the linear basis of demarcation. This longitudinal line can be pushed northward as well as southward. It can also be latitudinal with the Nile serving as a meridian.

4.8.1. The Disintegration of Sudan: the American Colonization

As this scenario of disintegration and American colonization is the one likely to happen in the South, it will be far more damaging as it may trigger off a Rwanda/Burundi style of ethnic genocide, because the linear polarization stops at nothing. The linear peace of the Addis Ababa Accord showed signs of this. Sudan is said to be a chromosome of Africa in its diversity. In fact each part of it is also a chromosome of the whole country; diversity is everywhere in Sudan. If the Southerners (as a bloc) have decided to pull out of united Sudan because they have come to the conclusion that diversity (as represented in regional blocs) is not manageable, what makes them sure that they can manage the diversity within the Southern bloc when broken down to its smallest coins? A watchmaker who fails to fix a grandfather clock can hardly be expected to repair a wristwatch.

This is also how Darfur is currently treated separately as a geopolitical entity in its own right with nothing to share with other marginalized regions of Sudan. The gruesome atrocities and genocide, which are being overtly committed by the state-backed pseudo-Arab militias, something that has so far been committed in the South under the cover of the jungle, have allowed the marking out of Darfur as a special case in its own right, but not as a natural expansion of the circular war. Such a situation will rationalize the international intervention, which was long since expected to develop into mandatory arrangements at any time.

The same can be said regarding the possibility of having the littoral region of Beja cut off. Within every entity of these regions new lines will eventually appear. The linear segmentation and polarization will stop at nothing. This is how Sudan is being sold piece by piece for the benefit of the neo-imperialism of western globalization, which is synonymous with western expansionism. This has been made possible by the vanity and stupidity of an out-of-date ideology whose futility will hopefully be discovered, when it is not too late.

The fact that the latest genocide in Darfur has been committed by Muslim Arabized tribes backed by the Islamo-Arab State against Muslim African tribes shows that Islamo-Arabism in Sudan is an ideological consciousness that has nothing to do with Islam. Those are Muslim people killing Muslim people with the intention of cleansing the land they live in from non-Arab people just as they did towards the African Dinka in al-Ḍiʿēn; the Arabs are killing the Africans - this is how they conceive of it in their twisted minds. Where the assimilation seems to be a cultural process, its parameters are racial. This is because centro-marginalization is based upon the processes of prestigma/stigma.

The leftist orientations of the marginalized people are not to be taken as victory, even when they succeed in separating their respective regions and assuming independency. Bearing in mind that they will probably achieve this with the political and logistical help of the West in general and America in particular, the superpowers will have them all dancing at the end of a string - just like puppeteers. It will surprise nobody if the linear segmentation continues to the point where we end up with Vatican-sized states run by the Americans, with two or three of them extremely wealthy with oil. The Arab sheikhdom monarchies of the Gulf are the most convenient model to follow. This is seemingly the reason to why the African fighters of Darfur have clearly stated that they are unionist in principle just like the SPLM/SPLA; no wonder they have named their movement the Sudan Liberation Movement/the Sudan Liberation Army (SLM/SLA). Furthermore, they have adopted the flag of freedom, i.e. the old flag that was raised on the first of January 1956, the one that Nimeiri in 1969 replaced by a typical Arab flag.

4.8.2. The Disintegration of Sudan: the Egyptian Colonization

Having the South, West and East cut off from the historical State of Sudan, with each of them going into internal linear polarizations, there is no guarantee that the so-called remaining North will be left intact. Taking Sudan as its backyard, Egypt will threateningly be furious about this disintegration unless she is given a big share of the booty. The occupation of the northern part of Sudan, i.e. the region of the Nile Nubians, had already been declared as a goal by the Egyptian officials in case the South seceded. Under the pretext of protecting its national water security, nothing will stop Egypt from annexing the Nubian region just a little upstream from Dungula. Egypt has already been occupying the two triangles of Serra, north of Ḥalfa, and Ḥalāyib on the Red Sea, more than two and a half decades. The triangle of the Nubian basin of Ḥalfa-ʽUwēnāt-Dungula is what Egypt is after; it will be annexed to the so-called Toshka agricultural scheme. At last, the expansionist nature of this move has dawned on the Nile Nubians. Among many memos of protest they sent, the first was addressed to the UN secretary-general and delivered at the Khartoum UN Office (cf. the Nubian Action Group's Memorandum dated April 13, 2004). In this memo, referring to the UN Declaration of the protection of minorities (Resolution 47/135, December 18, 1992), the Nubians asked for protection from the threats posed by both the governments of Khartoum and Cairo. Furthermore, they clearly identified with other marginalized groups of Sudan.

They have not yet received any gesture from the international organization addressing their problem. Aside from the marginalized groups already engaged in their respective civil wars, no political organization in the Sudan has so far made the slightest comment on the issue. The Nubians have raised the alarm, but it seems that the world is waiting for them to get killed in masses before paying attention, if at all. It should not be a surprise if we hear in the news that they have taken to arms. In that memo, the Nubians have extensively and persuasively explained their case. The memo has become a basis for their argument, from which other views have emanated.

The Egyptian expertise in micro-agriculture is well recognized, something they do not merit when it comes to macro-agricultural development. This is why international expertise has been invited to shoulder the task of developing the Toshka scheme. The Egyptian national contribution to the above-mentioned scheme is very marginal. The agrarian land of the triangle of the Nubian basin is much bigger than the developed area of the Toshka scheme. The Egyptians are in no way able to claim that they can develop the triangle of the Nubian basin in Sudan when they are unable to develop their own small project. They have neither the expertise nor the funds to do that. In fact, Sudan is more experienced than Egypt in macro-agriculture development. The big triangle of Egyptian colonialist settlement in the Sudan is aimed to extend from *Jabal* ʿUwēnāt at the border junction of Sudan, Chad, Libya and Egypt, to Ḥalāyib on the Red Sea with Dungula as its southern head.

In late 2003, news leaked out revealing that negotiations at the highest levels with the Egyptian government had taken place so as to facilitate the settlement of millions of Egyptian peasants, along with their families, in the triangle of the Nubian basin (Ḥalfa-ʿUwaināt-Dungula-Ḥalfa). Offers on behalf of the Sudanese government were generously made for a similar settlement in the fertile deltas of Tōkar and al-Gāsh, but were declined by the Egyptian party who seemed at this stage to be interested only in the Nubian basin. The aim of this move is said to safeguard the Arab identity of Sudan against the growing awareness *-sic-* of Africanism in Sudan generally and among the Nubians in particular.

The Sudanese delegation, which was backed by a Presidential mandate, was led by Arabist Nubians who belonged ideologically to the centre, but did not represent their marginalized people. A cover-up plan named the Four Freedoms, which theoretically allow the Sudanese and the Egyptians as well to own agrarian lands and settle in both countries, was officially declared. The cover-up plan has come out incompetently planned, as both parties were too eager in their scramble to create a de facto situation before the Nubians became aware of what was going on. There is no agrarian land to be owned by the Sudanese investors in Egypt. But there is land in the Sudan which the Egyptians are greedily looking to acquire. Millions of feddans in the Nubian basin were sold to the Egyptians with long-term leases, i.e. investment through settlement.

There is no mention of the Nubians in all these deals, which seem to have been made overnight.

What is suspicious is that certain Nubian organizations, then formed as NGOs, tacitly launched a campaign to nourish the faltering prestigmatic orientations among the Nubians. The then Minister of the Interior, General ʿAbdu al-Raḥīm Muḥammad Ḥusayn, who is also a Nubian, said in a comment on the Egyptian settlement issue while addressing a Nubian gathering in Khartoum in early 2000: "When it is peace, Sudan shall be dominated by the black slaves [i.e. people of the West, Nuba Mountains, Blue Nile, and particularly the Southerners]. In this case it is far better for us [i.e. the Nubians] to be occupied and ruled by the Egyptians. At least we shall end up blood-cleansed from the stigma of blackness."

The triangle of the Nubian basin was available for the Nubians to develop and settle in when the negotiations for building the High Dam began in the mid-20th century. That was the best solution as the Nubians could have continued to live in their historical habitat on the banks of the dam's reservoir (Lake Nubia) and agriculturally develop the Nubian basin. The Egyptians could have offered to supply the Nubians with power and water, if the welfare of the Nubians concerned them. On the contrary, the Egyptians wanted the area of the reservoir completely depopulated of its historical people (i.e. the Nubians of lower Nubia). Disrupting the Nubian society of Northern Sudan and Southern Egypt has been a target for the governments of both countries, as the Nubians constitute the only African entity on the Nile from Kōsti and Sinnār up the White and Blue Niles respectively down to the Mediterranean Sea. Furthermore, Egypt has had its colonialist plans for the Sudan for generations. The less populated an area, the easier it can be occupied.

The complicity of the Sudanese party in striking a quick deal shows in many ways of that suspicious deal - the Nubians are being sold free to the Egyptians. In the case of the High Dam, the head of the Sudanese delegation was enticed and made a winner in a set-up game of tennis with the Egyptian national champion, which intoxicated the military officer who nurtured a fancy for tennis. Swaying with euphoria, he went on to sign the betrayal of Sudanese Nubia in a meeting arranged immediately after the bogus contest. In the present case the price has risen a little – a top Sudanese football team was made winner in mid-1994 over a top Egyptian team in Cairo, for the first time in history. To beat an Egyptian team outside Egypt is commonplace, to beat it inside

Egypt is news. This is the reason why the Egyptians have never fared well in the contests of FIFA. For the last 30 years the football industry in the Sudan has been steadily dwindling. In this regard, Sudan has never been so far from beating Egypt as it is now.

The construction of a highway that connects Asuan with Dungula (i.e. on the west bank of the Nile) has been proclaimed by the Egyptians as a good-will gesture and for the benefit of the Nubians. As the Nubians are known to have about 70% of their settlements on the east bank of the Nile, the first reaction to that seemingly generous offer was to request the highway be built on the east bank, but to no avail. In fact, not only was the highway to be built on the west bank, but further was planned to be at an average distance of 20-30 km away from the bank of the Nile. It turned out that the Sudanese government was building it with Sudanese money as infrastructure for the facilitation of Egyptian settlement in the Nubian basin. At last, with the discontent among the Nubians growing up, the government decided to build a highway on the east bank of the Nile parallel to the one on the west bank.

The truth is that throughout history, Nubia (Sudan) and Egypt have been two separate states with the First Cataract at Asuan as a natural division and boundary. Occasionally, the material force of occupation had united them. Now to have the Nubian-ruled land occupied by Egypt means that the Egyptians have ultimately won a seven-thousand-year-old battle. If this is so, the Sudanese, generally speaking, whether united or disintegrated, will have nothing to glorify when they marvel at their ancient history and civilization.

The Nubians may play a decisive role in dismantling centro-marginalization if they have joined the struggle of the margin and have clearly identified themselves as an African marginal group. They have to bravely give the other marginalized groups the credit for pioneering this struggle, but they must also assure them that they will work very hard to merit the credit for being the factor sufficient to cause the swing. In fact, by their joining the struggle, the circle of marginalization around the centre closes in. In no way will their move to join and push forward the unification of the marginalized groups be taken merely as a political manoeuvre; it must have its roots in the ethno-cultural fabrics of the marginalized groups (cf. the affinities pertaining to the lingo-cultural phyla discussed in Chapter 1). The civilizations of Nubia, or Kush, have become an aspiration for blacks all over the world. The marginalized groups of the Sudan are rightfully sharing this civilization on an equal footing with the other Nubian ethnic groups whether they are in the north, Kurdofan or Darfur. It is high time that the Nubian civilization should have become an aspiration and a symbol of unity for the whole people of the Sudan.

Sudan is not that small, but what is small is indeed the clique of the Arabized elites that rule it. It is a gigantic nation led by dwarves, as Maḥmūd Muḥammad Ṭāha put it.

4.8.3. Sudan falls apart: the Centre cannot hold

The marginal people of the Sudan are pulling out, what will be left of present-day Sudan will amount to no more than the Nile strip of the 100% Arabized Sudan. At this point, it will become extremely difficult to distinguish between the centre as a centre of power, and the complete identification of the pseudo-Arabs of middle Sudan with this ideological Islamo-Arab centre. The people of the margin are in no way to blame for that. Failing to assimilate the different parts of Sudan by the strategy of centro-marginalization and the tactic of linear polarization, cultural reproduction, prestigma and stigma, the centre will finally be ready to do without them. Multi-culturalism cannot be managed by mono-culturalism. More has been bitten off than can be chewed.

In mid-September 2005, it was revealed on all Sudanese mass media that ʿAbdu al-Raḥīm Ḥamdi, the ex-Finance Minister, had presented a paper to the Economic Section of the National Congress (the ruling party) entitled: "The Future of Investment in the Interim Period". In the paper, which was based on the assumption of the falling away of the peripheral regions east, west, south and north of middle Sudan, he advises his party to concentrate on Kordufan and the middle Nile region, which he called "the axis of al-Ubayyiḍ-Sinnār-Dungula", i.e. what will remain of historical Sudan. His main point was that this region has achieved a great degree of cultural homogeneity with regard to Islam and Arabism, something he argued could be manipulated for the advantage of the National Congress, i.e. his political party. In relying on cultural homogeneity, the Nile strip remainder of Sudan is not to be hopeful of any peaceful prosperity either. A look at Somalia will show that cultural and ethnic homogeneity is not a guarantee for national integration and unity. The middle of Sudan is nothing more than the people of the margin being moulded and reproduced into Islamo-Arab culture. Based in essence on centro-marginalization, it will eventually emerge having its own linear stratification with its prestigma and stigma. centro-marginalization is like a black hole in the sky. It siphons the cosmos and itself into absolute nothingness. This is a cultural failure

– Islamo-Arabism has practically undone a history-long civilization of multi-culturalism and co-existence.

4.9. Sudan and South Sudan: the Long Path of Grievances

The war, any war, lived from outside is news whether good or bad; the war lived from within is a tragedy of bereavement. For four decades the Southerners have been living through continual bereavement caused by the civil war in Sudan. No one but God knows how the Southerners are coping with their eternal bereavement and noble sorrow that know no equivalent in history but the one created by slavery. More than two million lives of peaceful civilians have been lost. They have become a figure, two million, with no names or official records, let alone photos. The only solace we can have is that each one of them was missed and mourned by at least one relative. The infinite horror of this war could have been well conceived if it had been possible to collect the tears shed by the Southerners in barrels. As if this was not enough, the war spread to other parts of the Sudan. The only solace we can have is to achieve a true and lasting peace. By the turn of the century, comprehensive peace looked farther away than ever. This is how the Southerners had fallen prey to the offer made by the government of Khartoum to grant them the separation of the South through self-determination. Enough is enough! By that offer, the national statehood of the old Sudan was officially declared expired.

4.10. Sudan and South Sudan: the Path to Self-Determination

One of the tactics employed by the successive governments of Khartoum in this war is the manipulation of ethnicity to break up the unity of the Southerners. Many groups and individuals were manipulated to fight by proxy for the government. Their total vulnerability was the major factor forcing them into playing such roles. The SPLA has handled such cases with ruthlessness equivalent to that of the other party. This will never be forgiven by a considerable number of Southerners who will pose as the true representatives of the South. Those South Sudan nationalists have spearheaded the call for separating the South. Although it is part of the truth to say that this trend is the outcome of the manipulation of ethnicity by the government, nevertheless the role of the government in escalating the war has been decisive in giving it impetus. The separatists have always been there lurking behind the nationalist banners of the

Addis Ababa Accord and the unionist manifesto of the SPLM/SPLA. They came to centre-stage when the West directed its attention to the Islamic fundamentalist government of Khartoum with its infamous and fake *jihad* in the South, Nuba Mountains, and Blue Nile. Once self-determination was offered by the Islamic government of Khartoum in 1991, the separatists began working hard to have it recognized by the West. On the part of the West, it was considered too bold to insert in the agenda of Sudan the separation of the South in a straightforward way. Such a move is not only against the ordinance of the Organization of African Union, but also against the international law as self-determination is only recognized in cases of a nations' attempt to gain independence from colonialism or any mandatory state.

By that time the war had begun spreading to other marginalized parts of Sudan, with the SPLM/SPLA being either a convenient body to merge with and join, or to take as a model to follow. A few years later when the people of Darfur took up to arms to defend themselves against genocide, they named their movement Sudan Liberation Movement/Army (SLM/A). That is the time when the prestigma began working hard to contain the growing influence and leadership of the Southerners, especially John Garang whose formidable national image was becoming too threatening. The prestigma were not necessarily people affiliated to the Islamic regime; they were among the opposition also. Influential, non-partisan people among the intellectuals became very active in curbing the growing national recognition of John Garang. Self-determination for the South was put forward at an appropriate time; it did not mean separation, but it would definitely lead to it. The term was always expressed through the discourse and context of separation and independence.

In no time at all, once offered by Khartoum, it became very appealing to the Southerners. For many of them it caused euphoria. The history-long grudges and grievances were projected onto the dismissive arguments of many Southerners regarding any prospects of national unity. Adamantly and sometimes vindictively, they actually argued for the separation while pretending to talk about self-determination as if they were synonyms. To them, separation was like an achievement, replacing the lasting and humiliating defeat they, so far, had failed to inflict on the so-called North. On the other hand, the separatists also settled an account they had had with John Garang. It was either that he complied with the new trend and behaved himself as a Southerner, or he was going to lose the backing of the Southern public to whom John

Garang would look like a warmonger who takes Southern soldiers to die in a war that does not concern them. This was meant to bring John Garang back to being nothing more than a Southerner, just like them. Truly a prophet commands no prestige among his own people.

So far John Garang had stood firm against the plots of successive Khartoum governments to make him come for negotiations as a Southerner fighting for the South only. Ruthlessly, he had eradicated separatists from the ranks of the SPLM/SPLA. He also managed to manoeuvre around the pressure of America and Britain to make him fight for the separation of the South with assured promises of backing. But this time it looked as if he had been caughgt. John Garang could not afford to lose the Southern public, which supplied him with more than 85% of his soldiers. This was the paradox of his nationalist project; he was fighting with soldiers mainly from the South a war for the welfare of the whole of Sudan. The stigma was fighting and dying for the welfare of the prestigma without meriting its gratitude. This is too much for the Southerners however great a people they may be. Like ʿAlī ʿAbdu al-Laṭīf, John Garang had been let down by the so-called enlightened class of the Sudanese who, while admiring him and believing in him, lacked the courage to bring themselves under his leadership. There was no reason for that other than the mentality of the slaver's mind-set who expects the slave to die for the sake of their master's wellbeing. It was the last surviving trace of the vanity of the prestigma whose roots date back to thousand of years of slavery.

John Garang came to the table of negotiations with many cards up his sleeve. It was apparent to him that the Americans and British were driving the negotiations towards the separation of the South. Under the rule of the National Islamic Front (NIF), given its ideological bearings and corrupt policies, it was conceived as a matter of fact that the South would declare its independence from within its own constituent assembly. This was expected to take place within the first year of the Comprehensive Peace Accord (CPA) that was finally signed in 2005. That was the moment when John Garang made one of his breakthroughs that history will always recount. He demanded that self-determination not only be included in the treaty, but also be the axis of it. The Americans could not accept this. Danforth, its representative, counter argued that self-determination was redundant so far as the South will literally be independent, as they will be ruled by the SPLM. The SPLM could declare the independence of the South any time they liked with the backing of America guaranteed. However, Garang was adamant. If Southern Sudan was to become independent, then there must be a self-determination referendum. The Americans and British reluctantly agreed to this only to have another shock when Garang insisted that there must be a period of grace of six years before the referendum was undertaken. This condition brought the negotiations to a halt of almost five months with Garang stubbornly sticking to his demands.

Self-determination was a legitimate demand raised in bad faith by the Niavacha peace brokers. If it is only about separation, then it is simply a referendum that is needed. Indeed all marginalized areas are entitled to self-determination. But the question is: To determine what? The answer is to determine their rightful positions in the united Sudan in the first place. How? Through putting a package of constitutional and legal measures that will guarantee the welfare of the concerned region on one side and independence on the other. But to hold a naked referendum where people, who have been suffering for so long, are either to choose between the status quo or independence, is nothing but the sheer undermining of sovereignty. These were the basic agenda through which the marginalized people should have come to negotiate their project of self-determination. In such situations, an interim period where the central government is dissolved and replaced by a national unity government is deemed conditional so as to test the credibility of such a government on one hand, and to test the capability of the regional governments of the marginalized areas on the other. If all this fails to bring about justice, then the referendum is made as part of the self-determination package in which the concerned people should decide whether to keep in or to pull out.

These were the kind of ideas that stormed through Garang's brain. If the superpowers were determined to bring about the secession of the South Sudan, he [Garang] could not stand against it while armed only with nationalist arguments. Furthermore, he could not stand in the face of the growing pro-secession sentiment among the Southern public into whose sails strong winds were blowing from western mass media, in the USA and UK in particular (propelled by their respective governments and political lobbies). All these gathering winds were funneled and fanned out to the various Southern sectors through the heinous policies of the Khartoum regime that were meant to make the southerners believe in anything but unity.

Garang, a leader of genius at a very critical juncture of history, was the right man at the wrong moment. If he was given the six year period of grace, he was sure to secure the unity of the Sudan. If he was eliminated - as was prospected (by the Superpowers) – then it was up to the Northerners (government and opposition alike) to excel themselves and work hard to secure the unity of the country. If the regime of NIF stood as an obstacle (which was likely to happen), it would remain the responsibility of the Northern political forces to correct the situation to secure the unity of the Sudan rather than to resignedly rely on the political commitment of the SPLM with regard to unity. If all this failed, a matter that clearly implied the political and ideological stagnation in the North, i.e. to keep the status quo where the Southerners would keep living as second-class citizens in their own country, then the Southerners would have the full right to opt for secession in the upcoming referendum.

On August 30, 2005, the Ugandan presidential satellite-navigated plane boarded by Dr. John Garang de Mabior was downed by an unidentified superpower, by simply barring the satellite signals, making it a flying box. It is true that the weather was very bad and stormy, but not to the extent of making it crash in the Imatung mountains. Such weather was not going to bring that plane to crash on that mountain as long as there was enough signal to show it to its already computer-recorded route as that was not the first time for it to fly to the designated terminal.

After his tragic death, there was ample time for the NIF government to secure the unity of the Sudan if it had sincerely worked for it. On the contrary, they opportunistically seized on the departure of the leader to try to dissolve the SPLM by corrupting and dividing it. However, the SPLM stood firmly united against all the plots to divide them but not that firmly against corruption. They got infected with the virus of endemic corruption, a matter that would strip them later of their revolutionism both as a movement and as a political party. On their part, the northern opposition forces proved to be as imbecilic and inept as ever; it is claimed that the NIF is responsible for this inept opposition for its three decades of rule. But then what is the necessity for any opposition that fails to stand up as a potential opposition!

In June 2011 the South Sudan was officially declared an independent State as the Southerners voted in the referendum with an almost 99% majority for independence. The biggest African country of one million square miles, Sudan, had ceased to exist in that capacity. The history of the Sudan had never experienced such an upheaval. The ideology of Islamo-Arabism stands as directly responsible for this historic failure. The assumptions of the late Dr. John Garang have come true!

4.10.1. Liberation War or Leverage War?

It is worthy of discussion to indicate the level of revolutionary awareness among the fighters of the SPLA. As they were fighting and dying to build the 'New Sudan' they aspired for, the toll of death, disease and ordeals began accummulating and getting too much for them. As the 'New Sudan', when established, meant that all Sudanese people would enjoy living in it, a grudge was nursed among the ranks of SPLA fighters in particular and those of the South in general. This trend would get bigger and bigger the more the fighters and of the SPLA and people of the South got exasperated by what seemed to be unstoppable war due to the adamant mentality of the Islamo-Arab ideology mostly adhered to by the middle-north riverain Sudanese and governments (i.e. the centre). In proportion to this, the demand for separation kept growing and gaining momentum. The misconception here is that if you have to fight, then you fight to occupy your right place due to you as you conceive of it. A fight for leverage is tactical, not strategic; the fight for liberation is strategic, not tactical. This illustrates how the separation of South Sudan was mostly conceived by the Southerners as a penal measure against the so called Northerners, but not as a liberation project.

4.10.2. Is it politics or what is it?

In one of its definitions, politics is all about the art of achieving what is possible within the main guiding perspective of objectives. In the Sudan, where the majority of people living in the middle and north rivairin region mostly belong to the Islamo-Arab ideology (as this area is believed by many to be the milieu of the above mentioned ideology), history has shown over and over again that for more than a century those people have not so far awakened to the dire consequences of the ideology they adhere to. At last, the national statehood of the Sudan, which is built on the axis of the melting pot and assimilation, has reached its date of expiry.

4.10.3. South Sudan: Independent, but so what?

The independent South Sudan relies for 98% of its GDP on oil revenues. This means that the country, unless injected with aid cash, cannot survive if the flow of oil stops. The flow of oil means that there is a reversed flow of cash dearly needed for salaries, as there are no development schemes in South Sudan- so far. This is what the percentage of 98% means. The paradox is that this oil has to be exported not only through pipelines owned by the same villain government of

Khartoum, but also via ports in the same villain Republic of old Sudan. Even for its own home use, South Sudan has to rely on the refineries owned by Khartoum and situated in the northern part of the country. It is true that the SPLM was consumed during the period of grace by the Khartoum regime in exhaustively futile feuds. However, this can hardly stand as an excuse for not implementing any developmental projects in the South. The aspects of expenditure of the revenues of oil that were due to the South (billions in US dollars) have yet to be answered for. As said earlier, the SPLM leaders proved to be totally unready for good governance as they were infected by corruption. In the six years (2005 - 2011) the financial accounts of the South were not audited properly; although the Khartoum government wanted it that way so as to get them corrupted, the SPLM leaders proved not only easy targets but also showed an aptitude for corruption.

The major mistake, however, was to come to the Naivacha negotiations with a regime that represented the centre. Garang was fully aware about this liability. To him, the independence of the South was only an option when the worst came to the worst. Any negotiation by any marginalized group with the centre as a counter partner will definitely underline the recognition of the centre and its right to prevail. Paradoxically the demands of the marginalized groups can only be addressed by the dismantling of centro-marginalization. The precaution against such a pitfall is to take the dismantling of centro-marginalization as the parameter of any lasting settlement of the conflict.

The Southerners, as well as any marginalized group that reaches the point of implosion and gets compelled to take to arms, should know that in their noble fighting and dying they are not doing this to consolidate the prestigmatic centre. They are rather fighting to occupy the rightful position they are entitled to in the socio-economical realities of the Sudan. They are fighting against the institution of centro-marginalization in order to bring an end to the so-called prestigma/stigma institution. It is a battle destined to be won. After victory Sudan will be run by a government that owes its existence to the struggle of the marginalized people from whom the Southerners could have emerged as the leading group. This is the true war of liberation, not the leverage war. In the latter, people fight while counting on an assumption that the centre retains some wisdom to opt for lasting peace by correcting itself.

Opting for separation may be tantamount to succumbing by fleeing the battlefield. The blacks of America who emerged from the trauma of slavery provide us with a very telling lesson: those who decided to go back to Africa have not fared well by fleeing their historical battlefield. In fact they have ended up reproducing the vice of slavery on the actual indigenous African people who welcomed them back home. The result can be seen in present-day Liberia and Sierra Leone, where civil war had gone on and on with exceptionally very high records of atrocities. However, those who preferred to remain and face the dragon, ended up with a black person elected as president of the most powerful state in the world (Barack Obama). Indeed they still have a long way to go, but they are certainly on the right track. Martin Luther King's cry (I have a dream!) has come true. In the case of South Sudan, what does not make sense is the fact that separation has not guaranteed peace, as fighting and dying have continued with only one difference. This time fighting and dying are taking place between themselves for the benefit of global colonialists. This is the kind of short-sightedness that history never forgives.

South Sudan, the youngest nation in the world, has plunged into tribal wars led by the comrade-in-arms of yesterday. The atrocities of these infamous wars have made headline news worldwide. The other side of the tragedy is that the civil war in North Sudan between the Khartoum regime and the northern part of the SPLM was also resumed, with the two areas of Nuba Mountains in South Kordufan and the Blue Nile regions turned into open battlefields. As in previous leverage wars, now the call for self-determination has been voiced loudly in these two areas and has already gained momentum and will indeed consolidate in the future.

4.10.4. The Apartheid Republic of Sudan

The Comprehensive Peace Agreement (CPA) stated that in 2010 the referendum of self-determination for Southern Sudan would take place (it actually took place in 2011.) Accordingly a law for the referendum and its commission was decreed. For the first time, the phrase "Southern Sudanese" had its legally binding definition as the prospective voters in the referendum were to qualify accordingly to have their names registered in the referendum registry. Two legal conditions were made for that: 1/ any Sudanese (regardless of ethnicity) who had been living in the South for consecutive 5 years (2005 - 2010); 2/ any Sudanese living in the North but can trace their origin to the South. Out of about 4.5 millions Sudanese living in the North and who could have traced their origin to the South, only 160 thousand got their names registered. Once the sweeping result of the referendum was declared (99% voting for secession), Khartoum, against the constitution and nationality law, stripped the 4.5 million Sudanese people (who had nothing to do either with the CPA or the referendum) of their nationality on a racial basis. Thus, Sudan was officially declared an apartheid Southern race-free country (cf. Hāshim, 2014).

4.10.5. The Kleptocratic State of the Sudan

The National Islamic Front (NIF), a Muslim Brothers offshoot, which took power in the Sudan in 1989 by a military coup has nursed an extremely backward notion of the statehood and governance which completely belongs to the pre-national statehood. To them the nation statehood is condemned as heretical. Understandably they have never respected the institutions that make up the state. They have dealt with the state as a war trophy and began from day one to loot [*sic*] the government institutions and public funds.

On 24 April, 2017, the ENOUGH American organanization issued a report on the Sudan under the title: Sudan's Deep State: How Insiders Violently Privatized Sudan's Wealth, and How to Respond (https://enoughproject.org/reports/sudans-deep-state-how-insiders-violently-privatized-sudans-wealth-and-how-respond). The report begins by stating that: "Sudan's government is a violent kleptocracy, a system of misrule characterized by state capture and co-opted institutions, where a small ruling group maintains power indefinitely through various forms of corruption and violence. Throughout his reign, President Omar al-Bashir has overseen the entrenchment of systemic looting, widespread impunity, political repression, and state violence so that he and his inner circle can maintain absolute authority and continue looting the state. The result of this process, on the one hand, has been the amassment of fortunes for the president and a number of elites, enablers, and facilitators, and on the other hand crushing poverty and underdevelopment for most Sudanese people". Then it goes on demonstrating how Sudan now has become a failed state that capitalizes on conflict and corruption. The report says: "The system of rule by al-Bashir's regime in Sudan is best characterized as a violent kleptocracy, as its primary aims are self-enrichment and maintaining power indefinitely. To pursue these aims, the regime relies on a variety of tactics, including patronage and nepotism, the threat and use of political violence, and severe repression to co-opt or neutralize opponents and stifle dissent. ... It is this combination of extreme violence, authoritarian rule, and massive self-enrichment that qualifies the current system as a violent kleptocracy where state capture and hijacked institutions are the purpose and the rule, rather than the exception."

The revenue from oil never showed in the budget. It will indeed be very hard for many to contemplate the fact that the oil revenues of 2000 - 2010, which are estimated to have reached up to 240 billion US Dollars, were syphoned by the kleptocratic regime (cf. Hamid Ali, 2014).

4.10.6. The Vampire State of the Sudan

When every penny was syphoned in the draining system of corruption, and when every single public institution was either sold or plundered, the Islamo-Arab regime of Khartoum proved to be beyond the worst expectations. It showed another vice which is even worse than the vice of violent kleptocracy. That is the vice of being a vampire state (courtesy of my friend ʿAbdu al-Bāsiṭ Saʿīd), the first of its kind in history. The state began extorting money from the people by any means and at every corner. The vampire state has long since stopped subsidizing anything; the citizens must pay for everything they need whether food, health, education, housing, clothes etc. The state has literally stopped paying a penny for the public welfare for the last 28 years. Now with the oil gone after the secession of South Sudan in 2011, the kleptocratic ruling clique is determined to extort money from the people at any cost in order to enjoy the same luxurious style of life they were used to in the period between 1999 and 2011.

4.10.7. For how long can the marginalized people endure war?

The dilemma of liberation fighters in the Sudan is that they have to conduct their honourable wars within a social context of civilians. It is for the sake of those civilians that they have taken to arms and from whom they draw support and recruits. However, it is those civilians whom the successive central governments of Khartoum have targeted in a collective punishment for supporting the rebels. The tactics of scorched earth on the ground and continuous air bombardment are the most frequently adopted ones. Air bombardment continues to pour down hell on the heads of civilians, killing, maiming, wounding, and frightening them to death. Then the marauding army and militias will follow soon after. Villages, cultivation, livestock, and belongings are set aflame. Then the civilians are chased and hunted and put to the sword once captured. Then the girls and women are systematically raped and later mostly killed. The survivors will have to live with the shame and humiliation.

At this moment patriotism reaches its expiry date; the Sudan stops being a homeland for all its subjects. The seeds of self-determination are sown and eventually will sprout and become a people aspiration for those who are too tired of the de facto second class citizenship they have found themselves involved in without their free will. In the context of the national statehood patriotism should never be taken for granted. What aches deep in the heart is that after almost four centuries since the Westphalia peace agreement and the establishment of the national statehood there are people around who are mentally and psychologically short of grasping the essence of the all equal citizen-based state in which they are assumed to be living.

4.10.8. Self-determination as a Step towards Liberation

Self-determination is not synonym to separation as it can also lead to liberation. If wholesale liberation is deemed impossible, difficult or too costly, then other tactics should be followed, i.e. the tactic of liberation by retail, i.e. by piecemeal. Self-determination can serve as a point of departure for both separation and liberation. However, they do not go parallel to each other, but rather keep steadily diverging from each other. Where separation entails a cutting off of previous relations and pursues a completely independent road, liberation through self-determination cherishes the interdependencies and previous entanglements and all commonalities. Capitalizing on all these, the liberation-by-self-determination is strategically committed to the complete liberation and unification of the Sudan in the long run. Thus, any newly liberated area through self-determination will serve as a platform for further liberation movements whether they follow the wholesale tactic or the retail one.

CHAPTER 5

The True Peace

5.1. Know yourself: Africa, Unite!

True peace in the Sudan is a matter of common sense, long since lost as a result of cultural and racial prejudices. Prejudice is like snow, it melts slowly; in a context where prejudice prevails, common sense vanishes in the same way as a cool breeze vanishes with the weakest current of heat. Losing our common sense, we may not be lunatics but we are not fully sane either. The dilemma is that without common sense, the vanity of prejudice cannot be discerned, and with prejudice there is no common sense. When there is no way to break out of this vicious cycle, the only solution left is to exhaust prejudice by maximizing it: by war until people have had enough of it. And we have had enough of it! Isn't it time we regain our common sense?

People of the margin should come together. At the civilian political level they should have an alliance that represents their thinking. Before coordinating or uniting their military organnizations they need to have their civilian organizations united in a big alliance. The battle against the centre has had two fronts: military and civilian. So far the people of the margin have been faring very well on the military front, with nothing done on the civilian side. The two kinds of bodies are not necessarily to be conditioned by each other; although driving at one aim, the civilian battle, however, is radically different from the military battle. The Sudanese political middle should develop into its two wings: left-middle and right-middle. The right-middle should not mistake its position; it is part of the margin by the virtue of fighting the institution of stigma/prestigma and centro-marginalization. This alliance of the forces of the margin is fundamental in peace and war. If it is war, then war should be fought properly. If it is peace, then peace should be well guarded.

5.2. CUSH: the Alliance of Marginalized Forces

The paperwork and planning of this alliance had already been done in what came to be known as the manifesto of the Congress of United Sudan Homeland (CUSH). In the mid-1990s a group of Sudanese intellectuals representing almost all marginalized areas, began in Khartoum, under very difficult security situations, to formulate a manifesto that could serve as a political platform of a wide alliance for the marginalized groups. The draft - initially written by Abbakar Ādam Ismāʿīl, then a young man from the Nuba Mountains - was revised numerous times. The process of revision was in fact governed by successive consultations with representatives of marginalized groups. Although, no one claims that it has taken its final shape. However, it is claimed by many to be the most comprehensive treatise of its kind.

In 1999, a body called the Coordination Board was formed in which the marginalized areas were also reasonably represented. It was presided over by the late Muḥammad ʿAbdu al-Gādir Arbāb, a veteran politician and retired army officer from Darfur. At its first meeting, three landmark points were decided: (a) the name and principles of the alliance, (b) the types of organizations eligible for membership, and (c) democratization. In that meeting, the Pan-African nature of the movement was clearly manifested.

5.2.1. The Name and Principles

The name of the proposed organization, which is: the Congress of the United Sudan Homeland- CUSH) was unanimously endorsed. "Congress" was taken to represent democracy; "United" was taken to indicate the commitment of the movement to the unity of Sudan; "Sudan" was taken to show how this country has been associated with blacks throughout history, a matter that stands for both identity and continuity; "Homeland" was to represent the unshakeable belief of the movement in citizenship and national statehood regardless of race or religion. The principles agreed upon were: freedom, justice, and peace. There is no peace where there is no justice, and there is no justice if people are not free. These principles connote the relentless struggle of the Sudanese people for dignity, progress and prosperity.

5.2.2. The Organization

Three types of organization were thought eligible to join CUSH. They are as follows:

a) "Regionally-defined" organizations, such as "*Ittiḥād Nahḍat Dārfūr*" (The Union of Darfur Renaissance) or "*Ittiḥād Jibāl al-Nūba*" (The Union of Nuba Mountains) which respectively represented two different regions that contain various ethnic groups with legitimate demands in regard to development, identity and welfare. It was agreed that such organizations should bear the name of "*ittiḥād*" i.e. "union" in honour of the above pioneering organizations which, against all bigotry and prejudice, have normalized regionally-defined movements;

b) "Culturally-defined" organizations such as "*Mu'tamar al-Bija*" (The Congress of the Beja People) which represents an ethno-cultural group with its legitimate demands in regard to development, identity and welfare. It was agreed that such organizations should bear the name of "*mu'tamar*" i.e. "congress" in honour of such movements which have normalized culturally-defined organizations notwithstanding all the accusations levelled against them;

c) "Non-defined" organizations such as the Communist Party or the Muslim Brothers or the Sudanese Youth Union, which cannot be referred to or be posited in precise socio-cultural or regional settings, taking what they say of themselves by face value. No particular designation was suggested for such organizations.

It was believed that the cultural pluralism of Sudan would only be recognized practically when the inalienable right to form smaller organizational units to express the geopolitical and ethno-cultural peculiarities of this pluralism was also recognized. Belonging to more than one political organization is permissible as long as they are all CUSH signatories.

5.2.3. Democratization

"Grounded democracy" is deemed basic. It means democratizing the basic processes of decision-making within CUSH, i.e. between the signatory organizations and within the organizations themselves. For instance, in cases of constituencies where there are more than one CUSH signatory organization, the candidate to represent CUSH should be chosen through elections either confined to CUSH affiliates or open to all in the concerned constituency. This grounded democracy will teach the smaller organizations how to build coalitions within CUSH in oredr to have their voices heard. So instead of hypocritically denying differences, grounded democracy developmentally organizes and manages differences; those who do not tolerate this democratic game disqualify themselves from CUSH. In this way CUSH could go down to the people through their local organizations, while going up nationally. A rally organized to protest against slavery or massacres such as that of al-Ḍiʿēn at al-Ḍiʿēn area will concern only the local organizations affiliated to CUSH, while the same rally at the national level will concern all the parties affiliated to CUSH. It is this democratic and procedural dynamism that really distinguishes CUSH from other traditional and classical political organizations and coalitions.

This is why the manifesto is considered to be the most comprehensive treatise of its kind. It was written in a straightforward way that allows only those who really belong to it to come together. There is no way of either mistaking or confusing it with trends that do not belong to it. It bravely faces the crisis of centro-marginalization by naming and shaming. No marginalized group has so far claimed that its demands are not properly addressed by it or are missing. In the manifesto, reference was made to certain marginalized groups that were usually by-passed by politicians as they caused a lot of embarrassment and sensitivities, such as the Copts, Armenians, Chamese, Indians, Rashāyda, Fulani, Hausa, and Berno, etc., to say nothing of the so-called refugees from the neighbouring countries who had been living in the Sudan for decades and who rightly deserve citizenship.

Although the alliance of CUSH has not materialized into a tangible movement yet, the formidable political potential of mustering the forces of marginalized areas has been brought onto the political stage. From now on, different political groups will seek the building of such coalitions and alliances. In the period of the third democracy (1985 - 1989) such a coalition was declared in what came to be known with the name of "*Taḥāluf Quwa al-Rīf*" (the Alliance of the Forces of Rural Areas). It included a number of political organizations representing various marginalized areas. However, what it lacked was the vision and intellectual maturity regarding marginalization, a key word even absent in its name. The dire need for such an inclusive alliance of marginalized areas is easily discerned, as it could positively and effectively lead negotiations with the central government that represents the prestigma. Since 1989, it is usual that one or more opposition-marginalized groups are engaged in negotiations with the Islamic regime for peace and democracy. Peace can be achieved in one stroke and can be well-guarded against any relapse, that if all marginalized groups are united in one body. This will eventually push the right-wing to build up its own alliance as the prestigmatic right-wing will never fare well in the case that an alliance of the kind of CUSH is realized.

In the long run both the right-wing and left-wing will regain their common sense, a matter that will end up in them having compromised in the right-middle and the left-middle respectively. Not flanked anymore by its extreme extensions, the middle will split up into proper right and left, and that is the moment when Sudan will have its healthy right and left. A new middle whose identity is not very hard to forecast will eventually come into shape.

5.3. Federalism: dismantling Centralization

Autonomy is the essence of federalism. The different parts of Sudan have enjoyed autonomous rule since time immemorial. In the Funj era the tribal small kingdoms were autonomous. During the Turco-Egyptian colonialism, a policy of decentralization was adopted. During the British-Egyptian rule the tribal, native administration was a continuum of what had prevailed before. So federalism is a deep-rooted legacy. During the May regime regional governance (a different appellation of the same product) was introduced. Since then, politicians and regimes have employed a host of wordplay terminologies from Arabic to English and vice-versa. Nevertheless, the process of centro-marginalization has undone this history-long tradition of federalism.

Cultural centralism is the base of centro-marginalization. In such a context, technical federalism will amount to nothing more than a trick. Evasively, the concept of sharing power and wealth is being deliberated and then presented as the appropriate approach for solving the problem. As far as the process of cultural reproduction of the margin in the centre is going on, there is no way that a sound federalism can be achieved. Centro-marginalization defeats federalism. If children from marginalized groups would be humiliated in their early years in school simply because they do not speak Arabic, then what is the meaning of the federalism that stigmatizes non-Arab people in their own country?

The concepts of stigma and prestigma are embedded in the process of centro-marginalization. This is directly related to the problem of national character, personality and national identity. How is this going to be portrayed in our educational curricula? Lacking any vision pertaining to the cultural problem has been the primary shortcoming of the struggle of the margin against the centre. The Western model of superficially recognizing the blacks and other races under the banner of multi-culturalism, and having them on the façade of every cultural activity where the parameters prevailing are the mechanism of assimilation, is in no way to be followed. It has relegated the blacks in a similar way to slavery. Just like the marionette-slave, the Western culture of assimilation has yielded a very degenerate model for the blacks: to sing, dance and run. With such poor models it is hardly possible for the blacks to fare well; to sing, dance and run – as perceived by young blacks – one does not need to read and study hard. They only need to imitate. With levels of school dropouts and consequently juvenile crime on the increase, the blacks are being more and more stigmatized as good-for-nothing people. There is no way to allow this to happen in the Sudan, simply because this way the war is not going to stop.

The parameters of federalism should be the cultural premise and the cultural rights of all the people of Sudan. Federalism should be based on the perspective of unity in diversity, not that of the melting pot.

5.4. Plural Democracy, not Liberal Democracy

Democracy is not necessarily liberal. Liberalism is a western cultural characteristic. The liberal philosophy came into shape in the course of defending the individual's rights against violation by the state. Liberalism is individualistic by nature (cf. Mill, 1970). In the Sudanese society where the individual is identified according to age group, there is no place for either individualism or liberalism. Democracy is not a self-sufficient concept; it takes different shapes according to the cultural premise on which it is grounded. This is why the westerners have defined it with their own cultural identity, i.e. liberalism. This means that liberal democracy can never succeed if applied in a society whose culture is not characterized by individual liberalism. Shallowness is the least that can be said when one sees some of the Sudanese intellectuals chew the term "liberal democracy" without ever being able to swallow it. Moreover, it tells about the vanity of their democracy, which is nothing more than a technically expensive way of hassling people through the ballot.

Another cynical term also pondered over by some bogus intellectuals in the Sudan is the "democracy of Westminster". This is the democracy where bishops in the Church of England, not imams or rabbis, are members of parliament by virtue of being religious men with the right to vote. It is a democracy where the Queen is officially recognized by the state as the sponsor of the church. It is a democracy where the parliament is wholly based on two countering bodies: the Lords vs. the Commons, i.e. prestigmatic vs. stigmatic. The Lords are members by virtue of hereditary prestigma or at their best appointed. This is not meant in any way to mock the British system, despite the fact that many see it as deserving mockery, but rather to show how they have grounded democracy in their own culture according to their own ageless system of prestigma/stigma. How can our intellectuals use such terms in referring to the crippled democracy so far applied in the Sudan unless they are observing the prestigma/stigma similarity?

The democracy that can be applied in a culturally plural society is by definition pluralistic democracy. The premise of pluralism here is the various cultures. The whole culture of the group is equated to the individual in the Western democracy. In a society where the individual is asked for their tribe before being asked for their name, there is no individualism and by definition there is no liberalism.

5.5. Secularism and National Statehood

As said earlier, since its inception according to the Westphalia Peace Treaty between the Holy Roman empire and the United Provinces of the Netherlands in 1648, the nation-state has come into existence as structurally a secular institution as far as its power is drawn from the bottom up, not as in the Holy Roman empire from the top down. The treaty marks not only the birth of national statehood, but also the state with territorial sovereignty.

Secularism is generally held to be the separation of religion from the state. However, this extremely reductionistic explanation does not make sense as far as religion is nothing more than a certain set of ideas believed to be ordained from on high, and as far as the state is a collection of institutions developed by people in the course of history to facilitate the exercise of power for their own benefit. The institutions of the state are managed in accordance with the ideas held by the people who generate the power. In fact religion has never been separated from the state. What has been separated from the state is the religious institution, but not religion, generally speaking, or the religious ideas in particular. For instance, the church is a religious institution with its own differential stratification. The state could only become religious when such an institution occupies and then operates the state. Therefore the religious state is not only ideological, but more importantly is institutional. The religious state is not confined to religious thought and ideas; any religious group has the right to express their religious ideas and to further establish political parties. If these ideas and thoughts are democratic, i.e. not imposed or associated with any kind of harassment to those who disagree with them, then they are entitled to be the rights of democracy. If they are not, then they should be fought for being dictatorial rather than being religious.

Secularism in this age is a matter of necessity rather than an option. In a political context where the three powers, namely the executive, representational and judiciary, are integrally independent from each other, secularism becomes an unavoidable reality, even though a certain religious thought may be underlined in policy-making. As far as the ruling persons are elected by ballots based on the principle of "one person, one vote", regardless of gender, race, or religion, then the State is secular, because both the devolution and delegation of power are not governed by the internal mechanism of a religious institution. However, the religious fanatics may boast of having a certain religious orientation in dictating their policies. Religion has always been manipulated so as to justify oppression and political persecution, as is the case in the Islamic regime in the Sudan. More than dictatorial, the Islamic regime of the Sudan is also secular. Aside from the very backward regime of the Taliban and Dāʿish, there is no other Islamic regime in the world that cannot be described as secular. Needless to say almost all of them are dictatorial. Islamic thought will never do well in this age if it does not discover the secularism of Islam.

5.6. The Alliance of Marginalized People of the Sudan

In an African underdeveloped country, such as the Sudan, with the exception of a small sector, all the people are literally marginalized, provided that they become aware of their marginalization. The worst situation a marginalized group of people can find themselves involved in is that when it is not aware of being marginalized. The tool that falsifies the awareness of the people is ideology, by which they may nurse a completely false and erroneous idea about themselves. In the Sudan, where the Arabized black Africans (pseudo-Arabs) are the victims of such ideological falsification of consciousness, the Islamo-Arab ideology has made them live under the influence of the illusion that they are the Arabs of the Arabs.

The disillusionment and emancipation from this fantasy will make them discover their true African identity. This will consequently make them aware of how marginalized they are. Then the alliance of all marginalized people of the Sudan can be realized and implemented. Otherwise, there will be loop-holes and the circle of the margin around the centre may never close. As the Sudan is racing against time, the delay in this regard will eventually lead to the disintegration of the country, a matter that has already begun.

If the Arabized Africans of the Sudan proved to be so block-headed, the liberation and emancipation of the country will mean to defeat them along as part of the centre. Racism has proved all through history that it is reason-resistant. You cannot reason with racism; either you crush it, or it crushes you.

CHAPTER 6

Prosperity

6.1. Sudan: an Arabophone, not an Arab, Nation!

The true identity of the Sudan has so far been blurred and obliterated by the official ideology of the state. The issue of the identity of Sudan has to be revisited and reconsidered. Sudan should be recognized as an Arabophone country of black Africans. This fact must show in the discourse of the state whether in official statements, mass media, education, cultural aesthetics or the economy. It should be propagated that it is to our honour that we are black Africans. For the last five centuries Sudan has been run in accordance with the programme of mono-culturalism, thus overlooking and ignoring all other cultures. centro-marginalization, whether cultural, social, political or economic, has been worked intensively through the mechanism of prestigma/stigma which has created a reality typical of the Apartheid system. The cultural institutions of centro-marginalization and pre/stigmatization should be dismantled and abolished for good.

From being a leading country of civilization all through history, Sudan has ended up as a backward nation, or an invalid giant. Mono-culturalism is responsible for the failure to achieve prosperity. This being so, multi-culturalism should be recognized and practically manifested in all aspects of power processes; multi-lingualism must be recognized in education, culture and mass media.

Democracy has to be grounded on Sudanese realities of multi-culturalism. Plural democracy, not liberal democracy, must be based on our pluralism and multi-culturalism. Human rights and freedom of conscience are to be recognized by any politico-cultural movement. Political organizations advocating Islamic thought have the right to do so as long as they are democratic. In no way should dictatorship pass for Islam. The nobility of Islam must be saved from the degradation of ideological manipulation. The Sudanese armed forces must know their place and keep to it. The army has neither the right nor the qualification to act as an apparatus for governance. No military person has the right to aspire for political leadership until stripped of their epaulettes.

The right of the intellectuals of the various ethnic entities to develop and promote their own cultures and to express themselves politically, socially and culturally as representing certain ethnic groups should be recognized. The exercise of politics should be grounded on multi-cultural realities; any political organization has to be posited on certain cultural realities. There is no way for the melting pot nationalist parties to flourish, as they have all turned out to be representing the ideology of the centre. From now on, politics must not be exercised in the vacuum of this fake nationalism. The political organizations must openly declare their ideological inclinations, whether right, middle or left. The forces of the middle and alliance of marginalized forces must get united, as their unity will respectively accelerate the unification of the forces of the right as well as the left. In this regard they must enjoy the highest level of historical and revolutionary consciousness and clear vision that will eventually push aside the sleeper cells of the Islamo-Arab ideology. In the contemporary history of the Sudan, the winds of change fanned by marginalized people sufferings and struggle have never blown stronger than what they are now. If this will prove to be short of achieving victory, it is because of the reactionary role played by the sleeper cells of the ideology of Islamo-Arabism. The forces of the middle are in no way to aim to exclude the others; democratic co-existence in accordance with the principles of freedom, justice and peace should be their ultimate goal. People should be honoured with the due respect they deserve as human beings. However, the lines must be drawn clearly.

6.2. Pan-Africanism: a Sublime Mission

History tells us that so far prosperity has been the product of exploitation. The splendours of Western civilization cannot be viewed without consideration of the free labour of slavery and colonialism (cf. Rodney, 1972). Even the present-day prosperity of China cannot be viewed without considering the free and cheap labour it drew from its huge bulk of prisoners, political or criminal alike. All the wonders of ancient times that history tells about, the pyramids included, came to realization through exploitation.

It is only the Africans who are obliged to achieve prosperity without exploiting anyone. No one knows how to do it this way, as no one has ever done it before. Either we, the Africans, do it, or we are doomed. This is what unites us, Africans! This is what Pan-Africanism is all about! And this is why Pan-Africanism is worthwhile, because it is sublime. More than being the cradle of the human species, and the cradle of civilization, Africa is also shouldered with the historical responsibility of providing a case where prosperity is made possible without exploitation.

Without downplaying the consequences of colonialism, it can fairly be said that the failure of Africa with regard to governance can be referred in many ways to the fact that it is destined to do the impossible, that is to achieve prosperity without exploitation. It can be argued that our sanguinary despots are the way they are because the state policy of crushing the subjects is the most effective example history gives them. This is how advanced nations have maintained the rule of order. Usurping public funds is one of the legacies of yesterday's monarchies (even of many of today's third world monarchies) when the monarch literally owned their subjects. The advanced nations have had the privilege of learning from their mistakes (through trial and error), but not Africa—it is expected to succeed from the first attempt. This is why our failures thus far should be taken as our process of learning.

Sudan has the potential to set an example for other Arabophone countries and can serve as a model in maintaining unity in diversity for other African countries. Regionally, Sudan can make history once again by bringing the peoples and countries of *Bilād al-Sūdān* together with the peoples and countries of both the Horn of Africa and East Africa in a commonwealth and a common market, with an area on the Red Sea as a free trade zone with outlet lifelines to inland countries. Then after this, the other Red Sea littoral countries can be invited provided that they prove to be qualified to integrate with Africa rather than exploit it; the Arab countries meant in particular.

Understandably the neo-imperialist West will not allow such a thing to take place. Let us not forget that the underdevelopment of Africa was - and is still being - engineered by the West in general and Europe in particular (cf. Rodney, 1972). The West will do all it can to plot against such a step. Up to this moment, colonialist France compels the African Francophone countries to pay what it calls the colonial debt. It is money paid by these poor African states to France as a compensation for the 'development' it had implemented while colonizing these African lands and peoples. In fact, this huge amount of money, on which France has become quite dependent, is nothing but a ransom, or otherwise France will meddle further in the politics of these fragile countries. In some African countries, the so-called "colonial debt" was close to 40% of the country's budget. When the colonialist French left these countries, they plundered them, leaving them wrecked. What about the wealth France has stolen from these countries while colonizing them? This utterly humiliating reimbursement has been going on for decades now while Pan-Africanists worldwide are working hard to make the West recognize the Africans' right to reparation and repatriation.

Western imperialism will also do all it can not to allow Africa in particular and balck folks at large to have any more inspirational leaders like the forefathers and founders of Pan-Africanism. Below is a short, understandably not comprehensive, list of such inspirational leaders and what kind of fate most of them met: Felix Darfur (one of the early pioneers of Pan-Africanism who was executed in Haiti in 1822), Marcus Garvey Jr. (one of the godfathers of Pan Africanism who was framed, jailed and then deported from the USA; he was killed by betrayal and died in Jamaica in 1940), ʿAlī ʿAbdu al-Laṭīf (the great Sudanese nationalist and liberator who was betrayed and then assassinated in 1948), Patrice Lumumba (the first Prime Minister of the independent republic of the Congo, assassinated in 1961), William E.B. Du Bois (one of the godfathers of Pan Africanism; he died in 1963), Malcolm X (the great American civil rights activist, assassinated in 1965), Martin Luther King Jr. (the great American civil rights activist, assassinated in 1968), Kwame Nkrumah (liberator of Ghana and the first prime minister, ousted by a colonial-backed coup d'ëtat and later died in 1972), Amilcar Cabral (the revolutionary theorist and one of the greatest anti-colonial African leaders of the twentieth century, liberator of Guinea-Bissau, assassinated in 1973), Steve Biko (the great South African anti-apartheid activist, assassinated in 1977), Haile Selassie (emperor of Ethiopia, ousted by a leftist coup d'ëtat and eventually assassinated in 1975), Jomo Kenyatta (died in 1978), Walter Rodney (the prominent Guyanese historian, political activist and scholar, assassinated in 1980), Samora Machel (the first president of independent Mozambique, assassinated in 1984), Thomas Sankara (president of Burkina Faso, assassinated in 1987), Kenneth Kaunda (died in 1991), Melchior Ndadaye (the first democratically elected president of Burundi, brutally killed by a coup d'état in 1993), Cyprien Ntaryamira (president of Burundi) and Juvenal Habyarimana (president of Rwanda; assassinated together in 1994 by blowing up the plane they were on board while it was landing in Kigali), the liberator and father of the Tanzanian nation Julius Nyerere (died in 1999), Joshua Nkomo (died in 1999), Laurent Kabila (president of the Democratic Republic of Congo, assassinated in 2001) John Garang (Vice President of the Sudan, assassinated in 2005), the liberator and father of the South African nation Nelson Mandela (died in 2013), and last, but not least, Sam Nujoma, the liberator and father of the Namibian nation (living), to name but a few. Many of those who seemed to have died by health reasons were dealt tragic fates, orchestrated by foreign enemies and/or local traitors, almost similar in effect to physical assasination. Amilcar Cabral said at the funeral of Nkrumah: "Let no one tell us that Nkrumah died of a cancer to the throat or some other disease. No, Nkrumah has been killed by the cancer of betrayal that we should uproot out of Africa if we really want to definitely crush the imperialist domination in this continent." The imperialist conspiracies against Africa neither spared the Pan African thinkers, scholars, and activists nor the state presidents or vice-presidents.

Western Imperialism will do all it can to consolidate its hegemony over Africa. It is ready to destabilize Africa and weaken it in order to make it vulnerable enough to accept its hegemony. Such destabilizing movements as Boko Haram and other Islamic fanatical organizations are either directly made by Western powers or sponsored by them. From 2011, a series of news reports was circulated regarding the direct involvement of the Central Intelligence Agency (CIA) of the USA in the insurgences made by Boko Haram. The news indicated clearly the role the US Government in conjunction with its allies was playing to contain the growing influence of Nigeria in the sub-Saharan region.

Years back the CIA, while tactically taking advantage of the growing sectarian violence in Nigeria, recruited jobless Islamic extremist through Muslim and traditional leaders, offering training indirectly to the group by the use of foreign-based terror groups (see: http://www.nairaland.com/1202481/wikileaks-boko-haram-cia-covert and: http://newsrescue.com/boko-haram-a-cia-covert-operation-americas-destabilization-plots-against-nigeria-greenwhite-coalition/#axzz2LGP4WtOn).

Many websites tell how in December 2011 an Algerian-based CIA wing gave millions of dollars to Boko Haram. There is also the United States cable leaked by WikiLeaks on June 29, 2009 in which the CIA publicly predicted a specific deadly terrorist attack in Nigeria two months before Boko Haram started its terrorist operations. The websites also told how Boko Haram was financed; the US armed and financed Saudi Arabia who in turn armed and financed Libyan rebels that in turn armed and financed Malian rebels and Boko Haram. Ironically, this chain was disclosed months before Boko Haram began its terrorist operations. They also tell how the CIA was spying on Nigerian politicians by advanced eavesdropping devices and later blackmailed them. Software viruses were made by companies affiliated to the CIA programmers. To add insult to injury, the CIA pretended to cooperate with the Nigerian secret services when it was actually sabotaging the latter's effort to catch the agents of Boko Haram. In this regard, they point at what they call the "miraculous escape of Kabiru Sokoto" [then suspected of being a leading figure of Boko Haram] from a secret top security facility, the location of which was known to the CIA.

We can go on citing such websites, African and international as well, that revealed the relationship of the CIA with Boko Haram. But it is better we leave it here as it is available online worldwide. The collusion between the CIA and the terrorism of extreme Islamist movements, such as Boko Haram and Dāʿish, should not surprise anyone. The latest revealed documents by the American administration (cf. Exhibit 10 of U.S. Supreme Court Case No.00-9587, National Security Council Memorandum - 46, March 17, 1978. To: the Secretary of State, the Secretary of Defense, and the Director of Central Intelligence. SUBJECT: Black Africa and the U.S. Black Movement) shows how the US government can conspire against its own black population. The above-mentioned document shows clearly how the US administration looks at them as Africans, not as fully-fledged citizens. In fact there is nothing new in the USA foreign policy in particular and the West in general. To sum up, Western imperialism, as said over and over again, will do all it can in order to stop Black Africa from achieving a substantial degree of independence.

On the other hand, Black Africa is destined to first know its historical enemies, i.e. the West and any other imperialist power that may emerge from other spheres (such as expansionist China of today which is harnessing African states by over-loaning). Second, African states must cooperate between themselves to integrate. Third, Black Africa must succeed in solving its chronic problem of civil wars. Fourth, Black Africa must push forward toward real democratization so as to overtake the episode of dictatorship and tyranny. Fifth, Black Africa must rid itself of chronic corruption among figures and networks of authority. Sixth,

Black Africa must learn how to indigenize technology in order to catch up with the advanced world (cf. Shiekheldin, 2018). Last, but not least, Black Africans must believe deeply in themselves and that Africa will indeed prevail.

Africans must once again make History!

The equation is very simple: either you make history, or history will unmake you! However, no one who lives in the past can make history, especially those whose past- near or far- is full of misery and grievances. The history maker is a liberator by definition. And Africa indeed needs to be liberated and it is only the Africans who can liberate it. However, Africans must first liberate themselves mentally from the tangles of the past- not history! The past is linear and timeless while history remains full of time. History is neither linear nor is it about the past. History is a dynamic process of the space of time. It is more relevant to the present and future than to the past. History is all about how the present conceives itself as continuity from the past to the future. The historical consciousness is embedded deeply in the continuum that enjoys a good and resonant memory (past) and inspiring vision (future). It is through this that the present legitimizes and rationalizes its existence and consequently consolidates the future. History dies when it gets arrested in the past; the past is dead and will never come back to life. All the events that have not played any significant role in decisively building the present and paving the way to the future are long since gone and forgotten. The awareness of and about the multiple times dimension of history is the essence of human consciousness, i.e. of humanity.

When the Africans achieve this, they will be liberated from their past of misery and grievances without forgetting it. That is the moment when they become qualified to make history. The trauma of slavery, colonialism, and institutional racism of the past (and present as well) should transcended by a strong historical consciousness and clear vision that will return efficiently the stigma of all that to the real stigma, i.e. the culprit, not the victim. This is the only way for Africans to liberate themselves from the past while taking it on board. They must not wait for anyone else to do it for them, be it the United Nations, the International Criminal Court ... etc while waiting for justice to be done. They have to do it themselves by operating and leading these institutions and their likes. Either they do this, or they are doomed to the last moment of history.

Bibliography

- Ismāʿīl, Abbakar Ādam. 2015. *Jadaliyyat al-hāmish wa'l-markaz: qirā'ah jadīdah fī dafātir al-ṣirāʿ fi'l-Sūdān* [The Dialectics of the Margin and Centre. A New Interpretation of the Files of Conflicts in the Sudan]. Cairo.
- Abdin, Hasan. 1985. *Early Sudanese Nationalism: 1919-1925.* Khartoum: Khartoum University Press.
- ʿAbdu Allah, ʿAbdu Al-Gādir Mahmūd. 1985. *Al-lugha al-marawiyya* (The Meroitic Language), Jāmiʿat Al-Malik Suʿūd, [King Saud University]. Al-Riyadh.
- Abduljalil, Musa Adam & Khatir, Abdallah Adam. 1977. *Al-turāth al-sha'bi li-qabīlat al-Fur* [The Folklore of the Fur Tribe]. Khartoum: Institute of African and Asian Studies.
- ʿAbdul Mannan, M. Abdulsalam. 1990. The Resettlement of Halfawiyyin in the Butana as reflected in their Folksongs. Unpublished MA thesis. Khartoum: Institute of African & Asian Studies (IAAS), University of Khartoum.
- Abu Hasabu, Afaf Abdel Majid. 1985. *Factional Conflicts in the Sudanese Nationalist Movement: 1918- 1948.* Khartoum: Graduate College Publications, No. 12. University of Khartoum.
- Adams, William Y. 2004. "Peasant Archaeology in Nubia". In: *Azania* (Journal of the British Institute in Eastern Africa), Vol. XXXIX, 2004, PP. 111-124.
- Adams, William Y. 1982. "The Coming of Nubian Speakers to the Nile Valley". In: C. Ehret & M. Posnansky (ed.), *The Archaeological & Linguistic Reconstruction of African History.* Berkeley: University of California Press.

- Adams, William Y. 1977. *Nubia: Corridor to Africa*. Princeton, N.J.: Princeton University Press.
- ʿAfīf (al-), al-Bāqir. 2002. "The Crisis of Identity in Northern Sudan: A Dilemma of a Black People with a White Culture". A paper presented to the CODESRIA African Humanities Institute, tenured by the Programme of African Studies at the Northwestern University, Evanston, USA.
- Ahmed, A. Ghaffar M. 1988. *Qaḍāyā lil-niqāah: fī iṭār ifrīqiyat al Sūdān wa ʿurūbatuhū* [Issues for Discussion: About the Africanism and Arabism of the Sudan]. Khartoum: Khartoum University Press.
- Ali, Abbas Ibrahim Mohammad. 1972. *The British, the Slave Trade and Slavery in the Sudan: 1820-1881*. Khartoum: Khartoum University Press.
- Alier, Abel.1990. *Southern Sudan: Too many Agreements Dishonoured*. Exeter.
- Ali, Hamid E. 2014. Sudan Fiscal and Economic Crisis. A paper presented at Justice Africa Organization and Columbia Global Center. Nairobi Kenya. September 26 - 28, 2014.
- Awad (al), Ahmed (a). 1980. *Sudan Defence Force: Origin and Role, 1925 - 1955*. Khartoum University: Institute of African & Asian Studies.
- Awad (al), Ahmed (b). 1980. Militarism in the Colonial Experience. In: *Sudan Notes & Records* (*SNR*). Vol. LXI.
- Badri, Bābikir. 1955. *Tārīkh ḥayāti* [The History of my Life], Vol. 1. Khartoum.
- Barth, Fredrick (ed.). 1970. *Ethnic Groups and Boundaries*. Universitets Forlaget, Bergen – Oslo, & London: George Allen & Unwin.
- Battahani (El), Atta. 1986. Nationalism and Peasant Politics in the Nuba Mountains Region of Sudan: 1924 - 1966. Unpublished Ph.D. thesis, University of Sussex.
- Bekhiet, G. H. 1961. British Administration and Sudanese Nationalism. Ph.D. thesis. Cambridge University.
- Bell, Herman & M. Jalāl Hāshim. 2002. "Does Aten Live On in Kawa (Kowwa)? In: *Sudan & Nubia*, No. 6, PP. 42-46. 110.
- Beshīr [El-], ʿAbdu Allah al-Fakī. 2013. *Ṣāḥib al-fahm al-jadīd lil'Islām: Maḥmūd Muḥammad Ṭāha wa'l-muthaqqafūn: Qirā'ah fī'l-mawāqif wa tazwīr al-tārīkh* [The Propounder of the New Understanding of Islam Project: Maḥmūd Muḥammad Ṭāha and

the Intellectuals: Study of Stances and Distortion of History] Cairo: Ru'ya Distribution & Publishing House.

- Beshir, M.O. 1968. The *Southern Sudan: Background to Conflict.* London: C. Hurst & Co.
- Beshir, M.O. 1969. *Educational Development in the Sudan.* Oxford.
- Beshir, M.O. 1974. *Revolution and Nationalism in the Sudan.* London.
- Cunnison, Ian. 1971. Classification by Genealogy: A Problem of the Baqqara Belt. In Y.F. Hasan (ed). 1971. *Sudan in Africa.* Khartoum: Khartoum University Press.
- Bredin, G.R.F. 1961. The Life-Story of Yuzbashi Abdallah Adlan. In: *Sudan Notes & Records* (*SNR*). Vol. XLII. Double Number.
- Browne, G.M. 1989. *The Literary Texts in Old Nubian.* Wien-Mödling: Beitrage Zur Sudanforschung Beiheft 5.
- Burckhardt, J.L. 1819. *Travels in Nubia.* London: Murray for the Association for Promoting the Discovery of Interior Parts of Africa.
- Casati, Gaetano. 1891. *Ten Years in Equatoria and the Return with Emin Pasha.* 2 Vols. Tr. from Italian by: J. Randolph Clay and assisted by I. Walter Savage Landor. London: Frederick Warne & Co.
- Chinweizu, Onsucheka J. & Madubuike, Ihechukwu. 1980. *Towards the Decolonization of African Literature.* Howard University Press.
- Chinweizu, Onsucheka J. 1987. *Decolonizing the African Mind.* London: Sundoor.
- Clark, W.T. 1938. The Manners, Customs and Beliefs of the Northerner Beja. In: *Sudan Notes & Records* (*SNR*). Vol. XXI (1).
- Contran, Neno. 1996. *They are a Target.* Nairobi: Paulines Publications.
- Curtis, Mark. 2012. *Secret Affairs: Britain's Collusion with Radical Islam.* London: Serpent Tail.
- Ḍaif Allah, Muḥammad al-Nūr. 1985. *Kitāb tabaqāt al-awliyā' wa al-sālihiin wa al-'ulamā' wa al-shu'arā' fi al-Sūdān* [The Book of Classes of Saints, Holy Men, Scientists and Poets in the Sudan]. Ed. by Yusuf Fadl Hasan. Khartoum: Khartoum University Press.
- Ḍaw (al), 'Alī. 1985. *Traditional Musical Instruments in Sudan.* Khartoum: Institute of African & Asian Studies in collaboration, U. of K. with the Folklore Research Centre, Department of Culture, Ministry of Culture and Information.
- Deng, Francis M. 1973. *Dynamics of Identification: A Basis for National Integration in the Sudan.* Khartoum: Khartoum University Press.

- Deng, Francis M. 1978. *Africans of Two Worlds: The Dinka in Afro-Arab Sudan*. Yale: Yale University Press.
- Deng, Francis M. 1995. *War of Visions: Conflict of Identities in the Sudan*. Washington.
- Diop, Cheikh Anta. 1991. *Civilization or Barbarism: An Authentic Athropology*. Tr. from French to English by Yaa-Lengi Meema Ngemi. New York: Lawrence Hill Books.
- Fawzi, Ibrahim. 1901. *kitāb al-Sūdān bayn yaday Gordon wa Kitchener* [Sudan between the Hands of Gordon and Kitchener]. 2 Vol. Cairo: Muqattam Newspaper.
- Griffith, F. Ll. 1913. *The Nubian Texts of the Christian Period*. Berlin: Reimer Königliche Akademie der Wissenschaften.
- Goldberg, David M. 2003. *The Curse of Ham*. Oxford: Princeton University Press.
- Hai, M. A. 1976. *Conflict and Identity: The Cultural Poetics of Contemporary Sudanese Poetry*. Khartoum: University of Khartoum.
- Hamilton, James. 1857. *Sinai, the Hedjaz and Soudan*. London: Bentley.
- Hasan, Y.F. (ed). 1971. *Sudan in Africa*. Khartoum: Khartoum University Press.
- Hasan, Y.F. 1973. *The Arabs and the Sudan: from the Seventh to the Early Sixteenth Century*. Khartoum: Khartoum University Press.
- Hāshim, M. Jalāl. 1999. Al-Sudanu-ʿurūbiyya, aw taḥāluf al-hāribīn: al-mashrūʿ al-thaqāfi li ʿAbdu Allāhi ʿAlī Ibrāhīm fil-Sūdān" [The Sudano-Arabism or the Alliance of the Fugitives: the Cultural Project of ʿAbdullāhi ʿAlī Ibrāhīm in the Sudan], Conference of "The Sudan: Culture and Comprehensive Development: Toward a Cultural Strategy", the Centre of Sudanese Studies, Cairo, 4-7 August 1999. Opera House. Cairo.
- Hāshim, M. Jalāl. 2005. Islamization and Arabization of Africans as a Means to Political Power in the Sudan: Contradictions of Discrimination based on the Blackness of Skin and Stigma of Slavery and their Contribution to the Civil Wars. In: Bankie, B.F. & Mchombu, K. (2006). *Pan-Africanism: Strengthening the Unity of Africa and its Diaspora*. The Proceedings of the 17th All Africa Students Conference (AASC). University of Namibia (UNAM). Windhoek. Namibia 28th - 29th May 2005. Windhoek: Gamsberg Macmillan Publishers. PP. 244 - 267.
- Hāshim, M. Jalāl. 2010. The Dams of Northern Sudan and the policy of demographic Engineering. In: *International Journal of*

African Renaissance Studies- Multi-, Inter- and Transdisciplinarity, Volume 5 Issue 1, 148. http://www.informaworld.com/smpp/title~content=t777285704

- Hāshim, M. Jalāl. 2011. The Apartheid State of Northern Sudan: the Policy of Demographic engineering and the making of Civil Wars. *The African Writings*. An essay available worldwide at: http://blogs.african-writing.com/blog/archives/287
- Hāshim, M. Jalāl. 2014. *Manhaj al-taḥlīl al-thagāfi: Ṣirā' al hāmish w'l markaz* [The Cultural Analysis Approach: the Margin vs. the Centre Conflict]. 1st edition. Khartoum.
- Hāshim, M. Jalāl. 2018. *Manhaj al-taḥlīl al-thagāfi: mashrū' al-wataniyya al-sūdāniyya wa ẓāhirat al-thawra wa al-dīmugrāṭiyya* [The Cultural Analysis Approach: The Nation Statehood in the Sudan and the Phenomenon of Revolution and Democracy]. 8th Edition. Khartoum.
- Holt, P.M. 1963. Funj Origin: A Critique and New Evidence. In: *Journal of African History*, Vol. IV. 39-55.
- Holt, P.M. & M. W. Daly. 1988. *A History of the Sudan from the Coming of Islam to the Present Day*. 4th Ed. London. 111.
- Hureiz, S.H. 1966. Birth, Marriage, Death and Initiation Customs and Beliefs in the Central Sudan. M.A. thesis. University of Leeds.
- Hureiz, S.H.1977. *Ja'aliyyin Folktales: An Interplay of African, Arabian and Islamic Eelements*. Bloomington: Indiana University.
- Ibrāhīm, ʿAbdu Allāhi ʿAlī. 1989. Al-āfru-ʿurūbiyya aw taḥāluf al-hārbīn [The Afro-Arabism, or the Alliance of the Fugitives]. In: *Majalat al-Mustaqbal al-'Arabi* [The Bulletin of the Arab Future], 119, 1.
- Ibrahim, Abdullahi Ali. 1991. *Agāyēb: mūsīqa al-siyāsa wa siyāsat al-mūsīqa 'ind al-Hedendowa* [Agāyēb: The Music of Politics and the Politics of Music in the Hedendowa]. The Workshop of Traditional Music Manifestations. Department of Folklore. Institute of African & Asian Studies, University of Khartoum. Sharjah Hall. 5-7 February. 1991.
- Ibrāhīm, Ḥasan Aḥmad. 1971. *Muhammad 'Ali wa istikhdām al-ariqqā' al-*sūd [Muhammad Ali and the Use of Black Slaves]. In: *Bulletin of Sudanese Studies*. No. 1. Vol. III. pp. 95 - 109.
- Ibrāhīm, Yaḥya M. 1985. *Tārīkh al-ta'līm al-dīni fil-Sūdān* [The History of Religious Education in the Sudan]. Cairo.

- Jābir, Juma'a. n.d. *Al-mūsīqa al-Sūdāniyya: tārīkh, turāth, huwuiyya, naqd* [Sudanese Music: History, Heritage, Identity and Criticism]. Khartoum: Farabi Bookshop & Stationaries.
- Johnson, D. 2003. *The Root Causes of Sudan's Civil Wars*. Oxford: James Currey. Kampala: Fountain Publishers. Nairobi: E.A.E.P. Bloomington & Indianapolis: Indiana University Press.
- Khalid, Mansour. 1985. *Nimeiri and the Revolution of Dis-May*. London.
- Khalid, Mansour. (ed). 1987. *John Garang Speaks*. London.
- Kid (al-), Khalid H. Osman. 1987. The Effendiyya and the Concept of Nationalism in the Sudan. Ph.D. Dissertation, University of Reading.
- Ki-Zerbo, J. ed. 1990. *General History of Africa*. Vol.1 (Methodology & African Prehistory). Abridged Edition, James Currey, California, & UNESCO.
- Kurita, Yoshiko. 1997. *'Alī 'Abdu al-Laṭīf wa Thawrat 1942: bahth fī maṣādir al-thawra al-Sūdāniyya* ['Alī 'Abdu al-Laṭīf and the Revolution of 1942: A Research on the Origins of Sudanese Revolution]. Tr. Majdi al Na'īm. Cairo: Sudanese Studies Centre.
- Leinhardt, Godfrey. 1961. *Divinity and Experience: the Religion of the Dinka*. Oxford: Oxford University Press.
- Lepsius, K. R. 1880. *Nubische Grammatik: Mit einer Eileitung über die Völker und Sprachen afrikas*. Berlin.
- Lobban, R. Charles B. Rhoades, Jr. & Walid Bader. 1999. Rethinking Iron Working in Nubia. In: *Sudan Notes & Records* (*SNR*), No. 3 (New Series).
- Mafaje, Archie. 1961. The Role of the Bard in Contemporary African Communities. In: *Journal of African Languages*. Vol. b. Part 3.
- Mahmoud, Ushari & Baldu, S. 1987. *The Di'ein Massacre and the Institution of Slavery in the Sudan*. Khartoum.
- Mawut, Lazarus Leek. 1983. *Dinka resistance to condominium rule: 1902-1932*. Khartoum: Graduate College, University of Khartoum.
- Mazrui, Ali .1971. "The Multiple Marginality of the Sudan". In: Yusuf Fadl Hasan (ed). *Sudan in Africa*. Khartoum: Khartoum University Press. 112.
- Mazrui, Ali. 2002. *Black Reparations in the Era of Globalization*. New York: Institute of Global Cultural Studies.
- Mill, John S. 1970. *On Liberty*. London.
- Musul, Sayyid M. 'Abdalla. 1974. *Min turāth mantiqat al-Sukkout* [The Heritage of the Sukkout Region]. Khartoum: Institute of African & Asian Studies, University of Khartoum.

- Nagger (El), Omer. 1970. *The Pilgrimage Tradition in West Africa*. Khartoum: Khartoum University Press.
- Newbold, D. 1936. The Beja Tribe of the Red Sea Hills. In: Hamilton, J.A. de C. (ed). *The Anglo-Egyptian Sudan from Within*. London: Faber & Faber Ltd.
- Ohaj, Muhammad Adarōb. 1986. *Min tārīkh al-Bija*. [From the History of the Beja]. Vol.1.. Khartoum.
- Prah, Kwesi K (ed). 2006a. *Racism in the Global African Experience*. Cape Town: the Centre for Advanced Studies of African Societies (CASAS).
- Prah, Kwesi K (ed). 2006b. *Reflections on the Arab-led Slavery of Africans*. Cape Town: the Centre for Advanced Studies of African Societies (CASAS).
- Rodney, Walter. 1972. *How Europe Underdeveloped Africa*. (6th reprint, 1983). London and Dar-Essalam: Bogle-L'Ouverture Publications, and Tanzanian Publishing House.
- Ṣaghayrūn, Intiṣār. 1999. Asmā' wa maʿānī al-Sūdān al-qadīm wa dilālātuha al-jughrāfiyya wal-thaqāfiyya [The Names and Meanings of Ancient Sudan and their Geographical and Cultural Implications]. The 2nd National Conference on Geographical Names, the National Committee for Geographical Names (Ministry of Survey & Buildings Promotion) in Cooperation with Sudan University for Science & Technology, 6-8 April 1999, Sharjah Hall, Khartoum.
- Sanders, G.E.R. 1935. The Amarar. In: *Sudan Notes & Records* (*SNR*). Vol. XVIII (2).
- Sanderson, Passmore L. & N. Sanderson. 1981. *Education, Religion & Politics in Southern Sudan: 1899-1964*. Khartoum & London: Khartoum University Press.
- Sātti, Nūr al-Dīn. 1981. Al-ḥiwār bayn al-mukawwināt al-thaqāfiyya lil-umma al-Sūdāniyya [The Dialogue between the Cultural Components of the Sudanese Nation]. Part 3. *Mujallat al-thaqāfa al-Sūdāniyya* [The Bulletin of Sudanese Culture], Fifth Year, Vol. No. 17.
- Schweinfurth, G. 1874. *The Heart of Africa: Three Years' Travels and Adventures in the unexplored Regions of Central Africa from 1868 - 1871*. 2 Vols. Tr. from German by: Ellen Frewer. New York: Harpers & Brothers, Publishers.
- Shibayka, Makki. 1991. *Al-Sudan ʿabr al-qurūn* [The Sudan through the Centuries]. Beirut.

- Sīd Aḥmad, ʽAbdu al-Salām. 1991. *Al-fuqahā' wa'l-salṭana fī Sinnār: qirā'a fī tārīkh al-Islām wa'l-siyāsa fī al-Sūdān fī al-Sūdān: 1500-1821* [The *Fuqaha* and the Sultanate in Sennar: a Reader in the History of Islam and Politics in the Sudan: 1500-1821]. Prague
- Sīd (al-), Nāṣir. 1990. *Tārīkh al-siyāsa w'al-ta'līm fil-Sūdān* [The History of Politics & Education in the Sudan]. Khartoum: Khartoum University Press.
- Shiekheldin, H. Gusai. 2018. *Liberation and Technology: Development Possibilities in pursuing Technological Autonomy.* Dar es Salam: Mkuki na Nyota Publishers.
- Sikainga, Ahmed. 1996. *Slaves into Workers: Emancipation and Labour in Colonial Sudan.* Modern Middle-Eastern Studies No. 18, Austin, Texas.
- Simon, A. 1980a. *Nubian musik.* Berlin.
- Simon, A. 1980b. *Sufi Dhikir in* Sudan. Berlin.
- Slatin, R.C. 1898. *Fire and Sword in the Sudan: A Personal Narration of fighting and serving the Dervishes: 1879 - 1895.* London: Edward Arnold.
- Spaulding, J. 1985. *The Heroic Age in Sinnar.* Michigan: African Studies Centre, Michigan State University, East Lansing.
- Ṭāhir (al), al-Fātiḥ. 1993. *Ana Umdormān; tārīkh al-mūsīqa f'l-Sūdān* [I am Umdorman: the History of Music in the Sudan. Khartoum.
- Thiong'o (wa), Ngũgĩ . 1986. *Decolonising the Mind: the Politics of Language in African Literature.* Nairobi: Heinemann Educational.
- Ṭombol, Ḥamza al-Malik. 1972. *Al-adab al-Sūdānī wa mā yanbaghī an yakūn ʿalayhī* [The Sudanese Literature and How is it supposed to be]. Beirut.
- Tūnusi (al), Muḥammad ibn ʽUmar. 1965. *Tashḥīz al-azhān bi-sīrat bilād al-'Arab wa'l-Sūdān* [Refreshing the Minds with the History of the Arabs and Sudan Lands]. Ed. Khalīl Maḥmūd ʽAsākir & Musṭafa Muḥammad Musʽad. Cairo.
- Vantini, G .1981. *Christianity in the* Sudan. Bologna.
- Waddington, G. & B. Hanbury. 1822. *Journals of a Visit to Some Parts of Ethiopia.* London.
- Welsby, D. ed. 2000. *Life on the Desert Edge: Seven Thousands Years of Settlement in the Northern Dongola Reach of the Nile.* London: Sudan Archaeological Research society.
- Werner, R., William Anderson & Andrew Wheeler. 2000. *Day of Devastation, Day of Contentment: the History of the Sudanese Church across 2000 years.* Nairobi: Paulines Publications Africa.

- Wyndham, R. 1937. *The Gentle Savage: A Sudanese Journey in the Province of Bahr-el Ghazal, commonly called 'Bog'*. 4th ed. London: Cassell & Company, Ltd.
- Yamauchi, E. 2004. *Africa and the Bible*. Michigan: Baker Academic.

Primary Sources

- Amilcar Cabral: (The Cancer of Betrayal). May 13, 1972: https://www.youtube.com/watch?v=rLo3Y2IG-iY
- Amnesty International. 2017. *Libya's Dark Web of Collusion: Abuses Against Europe-bound Refugees and Migrants*. London: Amnesty International.
- Baṣri (al), 'Āyisha. 2014. The Report of the Sposkeswoman of UNAMID on the complicity of UNAMID with the governemnt of Sudan, In: *Foreign Policy Magazine*, 9 April 2014.
- Klaas van Dijken. 2018. Rijke Syrische vluchtelingen reizen naar Europa via Soedan, met een illegaal Soedanees paspoort. In: Trouw. 12 April 2018: https://www.trouw.nl/samenleving/waarom-rijke-syrische-vluchtelingen-via-soedan-naar-europa-reizen~ab331b31/
- Egypt minister insults Africans Read more: https://tuko.co.ke/134967-drama-un-nairobi-egypt-minister-calls-africans-dogs-slaves.html
- ENOUGH organanization Report on the Sudan (24 April 2017): Sudan's Deep State: How Insiders Violently Privatized Sudan's Wealth, and How to Respond: https://enoughproject.org/reports/sudans-deep-state-how-insiders-violently-privatized-sudans-wealth-and-how-respond
- (The) EU dealing with the Sudan to curb Migration. In: The Sunday Express (May 15, 2016): http://www.express.co.uk/news/world/670550/EU-secret-deal-war-criminal-Sudan-migrant-crisis-Africa
- Group Rape in Tabit Village, Darfur. New York, The Statement attributable to the Spokesman for the Secretary-General on Darfur, 17 November 2014: http://www.UN.org/sg/statements/index.asp?NID=8196
- Kingsley, Patrick. 2018. "By Stifling Migration, Sudan's Feared Secret Police Aid Europe". The New York Times. 22 April 2018: https://www.nytimes.com/2018/04/22/world/africa/migration-european-union-sudan.html
- Lincoln, Abraham (1858), "Lincoln-Douglas debates, 1858": www.founding.com

- (The) Manifesto of Congress of United Sudan Homeland (CUSH).
- (The) National Security Council Memorandum - 46, March 17, 1978. Exhibit 10 of U.S. Supreme Court Case No.00-9587, To: the Secretary of State, the Secretary of Defense, and the Director of Central Intelligence. SUBJECT: Black Africa and the U.S. Black Movement.
- (The) Nubian Action Group (2004) "The Government of Khartoum sells out its Nubian Subjects and their Land", Memorandum to Kofi Annan, the Secretary-General of the United Nations, April 13, 2004, Khartoum.
- *(Al-)Nahār Kuwaiti Newspaper*. 2018. The [Kuwaiti] Stateless: a Safe Sector and Sudanese Passports. 10 March 2018.
- People for Sale: Exposing Migrant Slave Auctions in Libya. CNN: https://edition.cnn.com/specials/africa/libya-slave-auctions
- Summer Institute of Linguistics: www.ethnologue.org

Printed in the United States
By Bookmasters